Listening Plus

Authentic recordings with tasks to develop listening skills and learner training

Student's Book

John McDowell
Christopher Hart

Nelson

Cartoons by Matthew Doyle.
Front Cover photographs by Steve Richards and Donna Thynne.

The Publishers would like to thank Barraq Ali, Julia Dall, Ken and Philippa Khoo, and Masai Marr for being photographed for the front cover.

Thomas Nelson and Sons Ltd
Nelson House Mayfield Road
Walton-on-Thames Surrey
KT12 5PL UK

51 York Place
Edinburgh
EH1 3JD UK

Thomas Nelson (Hong Kong) Ltd
Toppan Building 10/F
22A Westlands Road
Quarry Bay Hong Kong

First published by Edward Arnold (Publishers) Ltd 1987. Reprinted 1988.
ISBN 0-7131-8448-5

This edition published by Thomas Nelson and Sons Ltd 1991
ISBN 0-17-556150-8
NPN 9 8 7 6 5 4 3 2

Printed and bound in Great Britain by M & A Thomson Litho, East Kilbride.

Contents

Introduction

What is *Listening Plus*?

It is a course consisting of a student's book, a teacher's book and a cassette, designed to train intermediate learners to listen effectively to English spoken at normal speed.

What is listening?

We can analyse listening into a series of sub-skills and strategies that we use at different times depending on what we are listening to and why. What we listen to includes radio, television news, people talking to us, people talking to each other, and announcements. Our reasons for listening include listening for a specific piece of information, listening for general meaning, listening for the speaker's attitude, and listening for pleasure. By practising different listening strategies and sub-skills such as prediction skills, inference skills, listening for key words, listening for specific information, using our previous knowledge etc., we can develop the ability to listen effectively.

What does *Listening Plus* do?

1. It helps you to understand everyday spoken English by developing listening sub-skills.
2. It integrates listening with speaking, with reading, and with writing.
3. It encourages you to look at methods of learning and to develop strategies which will help you to learn more effectively.

How do you use *Listening Plus?*

First do Unit 0, Handy Hints. It is an introductory unit and gives you guidelines on how to listen effectively and on how to use the material in this book. If you find the recorded material in this unit difficult to understand, do not worry! The unit is designed to prove to you that you can understand even the most difficult authentic discourse if you learn how to listen effectively. The tasks have not been designed to test you, but to help you to build up an understanding of the recordings.

When you have done Unit 0, you can then work through the other units in the order you choose. As you do them, remember what you read in Unit 0: that the tasks are organised in such a way that they will help you to build up understanding of the recorded texts little by little. You will probably not find the material in these units as hard as that in Unit 0, however.

What does each unit consist of?

In each unit you will normally find:

- pre-listening task(s) to familiarise you with the topic of the unit and to help you to anticipate some of the information and language that you will hear on the tape.
- task(s) to help you to focus on the main ideas of the recordings.
- task(s) which will help you to listen more intensively and to focus on specific information or on language forms.
- related activities to link listening with other skills.

In most units you will be encouraged to think about learning in general and about your learning in particular. The objective is to help you to develop the learning style that works best for you.

Unit 0 Handy Hints

What I find difficult is if someone talks to me unexpectedly. In the middle of a conversation where I know the topic, it's all right.

The aim of this unit is to introduce *Listening Plus* and to give you some hints on how to make listening to English easier.

1 Think about the problems you have when you listen to spoken English. Try to specify what it is that causes difficulty, and make a list. The comments on the left-hand side of this page, made by English people studying a foreign language, might help you to remember some of your own problems.

Sometimes I just get tired and stop listening. People speak so fast and it is a strain to listen.

I wish people would pause occasionally. It would give me time to think and work things out.

2 All the material on the tape accompanying *Listening Plus* is authentic language in the sense that it has not been simplified or slowed down and there are a lot of different speakers and accents. You may find, then, that when you use *Listening Plus* you will meet some of the difficulties that you have just mentioned. However, the tasks in the book are designed to help you get over the difficulties and to give you practice in understanding 'real' English as it is normally spoken. Here are some hints to make it easier. Because the material on the tape is authentic, you might find that the people seem to talk very fast and that you have difficulty catching every word. Don't worry! Most people do not even try to listen for every word when they listen in their own language. Instead, they tend to listen out for the main words that give clues to what the message is about and then supply the rest themselves from what they already know.

When I know what people are talking about, it's quite simple. I can follow the main ideas and just fill in the rest by guessing.

3 **a** Listen to Ruth and Nigel chatting. What they are talking about is not absolutely clear, but they keep repeating a word that gives us a good clue to what it might be. What is the word? And what do you think they are talking about (you might think of more than one possibility)?

b Now listen to the rest of the conversation. You should now be able to identify the exact topic of their conversation. Make a note of all the words that help you.

I find it easier when the person is talking only to me. If there is a group of people talking, I get lost.

You probably couldn't hear every single word that Ruth and Nigel said, but you know what their conversation was about. What you did was to use all the words you did understand, together with what you know about sport, to help you get at the meaning. Try to do this when you work with the other tasks in *Listening Plus*. Listen out for key words and use all the other information you have to make guesses about what the meaning of the conversations could be.

4 Here is a more difficult example of listening for clues. Alison is at a dinner party. Listen and try to guess what she is talking about. Make a note of the words that give you clues. You might not feel very certain but you can make good guesses.

Now look at these pictures. Do they help you? Which one do you think corresponds to what Alison is saying?

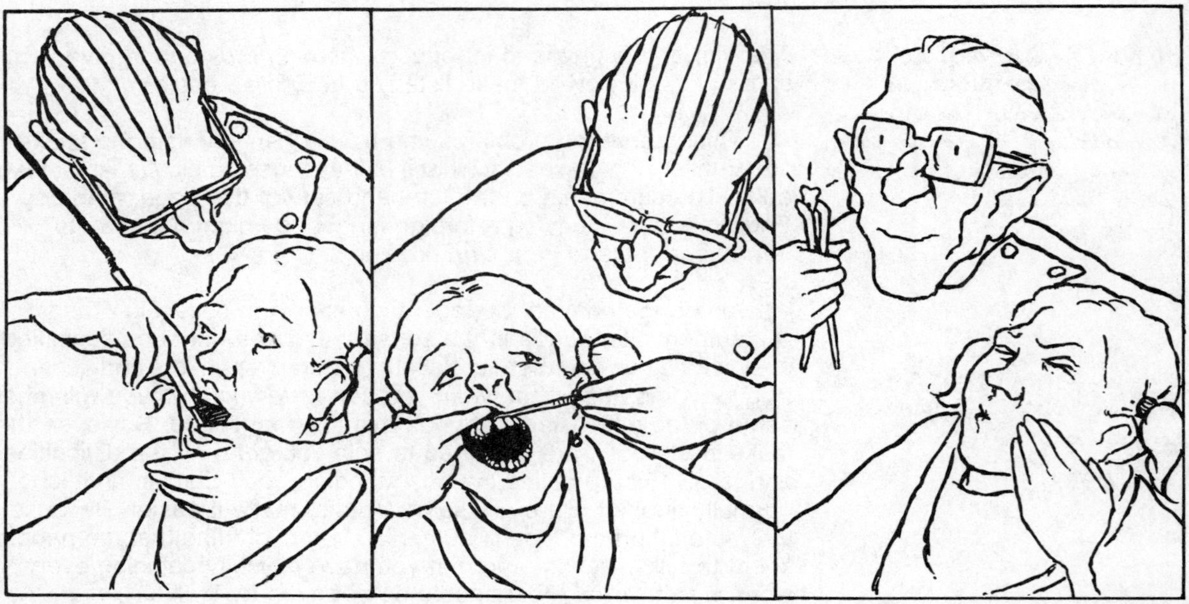

1 2 3

Listen to the tape again and try to get more details. First, read these questions, and try to answer them as you listen. Use some of these words in your answers: **rubber band**, **metal ring**, **wire**, **stuck out**, **zig-zag**.

a When did the experience she describes occur?

b Why?

c What was done to her teeth?

d How long did it last?

Here, you found out little by little what the conversation was about by listening again and again, each time with a few more clues to help you. As you gained more information, it should have been easier to make sense of what Alison was saying. Remember this when you do the other tasks in this book. Listen to the tape as many times as you like and build on any information you have.

5 Now here is something more difficult. You are going to hear an extract from which most of the words have been removed and only the key words left.

First, look at the drawing at the top of the next page. What would you expect the tape that accompanies it to be about?

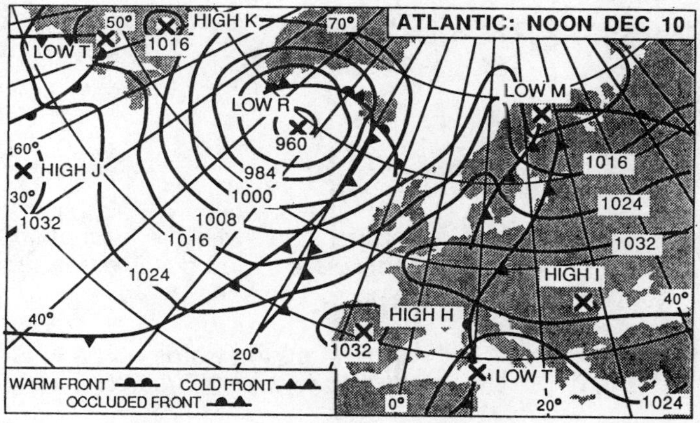

Now listen to the tape, most of which has been erased, and answer these questions.

- **a** What is the weather like now?
- **b** What will it be like tonight?
- **c** What will it be like early tomorrow morning?

Even though a lot of the extract was in fact missing, you were probably able to answer all the above questions. You were able to take the key words that were left and to guess the rest from what you already know about weather forecasts in general and what you expect to hear on them. This confirms the value of the kind of task you were doing when you were listening to Nigel and Ruth and to Alison.

So, here are two pieces of advice for using this book and the cassette.

- Do all the anticipation exercises which are there to help you focus on the topic and build up your expectations.
- Do not try to listen for every word and do not worry if there are things that you do not understand. Focus on what you can understand and use that to build up the message. Then, when you have got the general message, you can go back and try to understand more if you feel that you want to.

6 Here is another kind of task which involves using information to guess what someone is saying. Often, when you are in a room with someone who is talking on the telephone, you can guess what the person at the other end of the line is saying. Tina was at the same dinner party as Alison, and after the meal she made this telephone call. Listen and try to work out what the other person is saying.

- First listen straight through to get the general idea.
- Then listen again and try to write down what you think the other person is saying.

7 Now do the same with the following conversation. John is making a telephone call.

8 Now look back at the list of difficulties you compiled in task 1. Have you found any ways of solving some of them?

Unit 1 Storeys From Spain

This unit deals with the description of buildings. You will hear different people describing buildings and then you will be able to practise doing so yourself.

1 **a** Use the words below to label different parts of the buildings beside them. If you can, work with a partner.

flat roof
arches
pillar
turret
sloping roof
ground floor

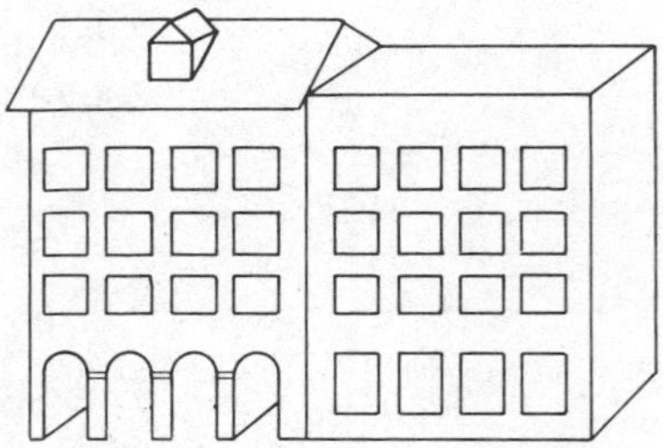

b What other words would you need if someone asked you to describe these buildings? Make a list. Again, if you can, work with a partner.

2 This is a photograph of the main square in Vic, a town in Catalonia in the north-east of Spain. On the tape, you will hear different people describing buildings in the square. Listen and decide which building each person is describing. (There are six people but some of them describe the same building.)
The people you hear are:

1 Peter
2 Alison
3 Nigel
4 Brenda
5 Elizabeth
6 Deborah

3 It is sometimes difficult to describe things very exactly, so we often use expressions like:

It *seems to be* a hotel.
It *looks as though it is* a hotel.

These express a degree of uncertainty or tentativeness. The people on the tape all use similar expressions with the verbs 'to seem' or 'to look'. Listen again and write down the expressions you hear. (You should try to write down one expression for each person.) How do the expressions differ?

4 Work in pairs or small groups and look at the photograph of Vic. Take it in turns to choose a building and describe it while the others try to guess which one you are describing. Use the language from task 3 if you need to.

5 The people you listened to on the tape qualified their comments on the different buildings. They did this by using adverbs of degree to modify the adjectives they chose to describe the buildings.

For example: '*very* ugly'.

Listen to the tape again and write down all the different adverbs you hear which modify adjectives. Try to find five.

6 Apart from the expressions you noted in task 3, Deborah uses different ways of describing something that she cannot be exact about.

For example: 'It's got a *kind of* open gallery . . .
It *looks sort of* Dutch 17th century
. . . a *very-difficult-to-describe kind of* structure . . .
. . . a *Dutch-looking* little building . . .'

Listen to her again and make sure you understand how she uses these expressions.

7 Now use some of the expressions in task 6 to describe this photograph.

Unit 2 Phobias

This unit is about common fears and anxieties. You will hear different people talking about the things which frighten them and, if you want to, you will be able to talk about the things which bother you.

1 Look at the words and expressions in the box below and classify them according to whether they are:

strong **quite strong** **not so strong**

phobia (n)	**anxiety** (n)	**uneasiness** (n)
afraid of (adj)	**terrified of** (adj)	**petrified of** (adj)
can't stand (v)	**hate** (v)	**makes me feel uneasy**

2 Listen to these five people talking about things which frighten them. What exactly is each person afraid of?

1 Donald
2 Pat
3 Tina
4 Mike
5 Deborah

3 Can you think of any things that people are afraid of? Make a list of those you have noticed. If possible, work in pairs or small groups.

4 Now listen to Dr John Hart, a psychiatrist, talking about fears and anxieties. Read the following questions and dictionary extract before you listen to the tape.

a How does Dr Hart define a phobia? Is his definition the same as this one from the Penguin Dictionary of Psychology?

phobia A term from the Greek for *fear* or *dread*; in keeping with this etymology, specific phobias are properly given Greek root qualifiers, e.g., *pyrophobia* = fear of fire, *nyctophobia* = fear of the night, etc. In standard psychiatric work, a reaction requires several factors before it is properly classified as a phobia. Specifically, the fear must be persistent and intense, there must be a compelling need to flee or avoid the phobic object or situation and the fear must be irrational and not based on sound judgement. ◊ *phobic disorder* for some additional points on the contemporary classification scheme.

phobia, simple An umbrella term for any ◊ *phobic disorder* associated with a relatively well-defined (i.e. "simple") stimulus. Most phobias other than ◊ *agoraphobia* and the ◊ *social *phobias* are included here.

b Which of the five people you listened to in task 2 may not have a phobia? Give reasons for your answer.

5 Now listen to Dr Hart defining three types of phobia. Read the following questions before you listen.

a What are the three types of phobia?

b Classify the five cases from task 2 according to type.

6 The psychiatrist goes on to talk about 'free-floating anxiety'. Read the following questions before you listen to him.

a What is 'free-floating anxiety'?

b How do people tolerate 'free-floating anxiety'?

c Which of the five cases from task 2 may be explained in this way?

7 There are several ways of treating people with phobias. Here, Dr Hart discusses the most popular way. Read the following tasks, and then listen to the tape.

a List the stages in the treatment of someone who is afraid of spiders.

b Choose one of the five cases we have heard about and explain how this method may be applied.

8 Read this extract from *Nineteen eighty-four* by George Orwell. When you have read it, talk about how you felt or what sensations you had as you read it.

> "You asked me once," said O'Brien, "what was in Room 101. I told you that you knew the answer already. Everyone knows it. The thing that is in Room 101 is the worst thing in the world."
>
> The door opened again. A guard came in carrying something made of wire, a box or basket of some kind. He set it down on the further table. Because of the position in which O'Brien was standing, Winston could not see what the thing was.
>
> "The worst thing in the world," said O'Brien, "varies from individual to individual. It may be burial alive, or death by fire, or by drowning or by impalement, or fifty other deaths. There are cases where it is some quite trivial thing, not even fatal."
>
> He had moved a little to one side, so that Winston had a better view of the thing on the table. It was an oblong wire cage with a handle on top for carrying it by. Fixed to the front of it was something that looked like a fencing mask, with the concave side outwards. Although it was three or four metres away from him, he could see that the cage was divided lengthways into two compartments, and that there was some kind of creature in each. They were rats.
>
> "In your case," said O'Brien, "the worst thing in the world happens to be rats."

9 Not long after these recordings were made, Deborah, to whom you listened in task 2, went to a seminar to try to get over her fear of flying. She wrote to tell us about it. Read her letter and then do the followng tasks.

a Make a note of the different things she did at the seminar and how she felt about each one.

b Compare the seminar with the treatment that Dr Hart described in task 7.

Dear John,

Just a quick note to tell you about the flying phobia seminar and its results. Three fearful fliers met at Guy's Hospital and were first asked to talk about past experiences and present fears. We then listened to the psychologist explaining why a plane stays up in the air, followed by some deep breathing exercises – all nice and easy. The afternoon was spent in the "flight simulator", an ingenious mock-up of the interior of a plane, with a video'ed take-off and landing. This was very realistic and somewhat distressing for all of us. However, we all turned up at Heathrow Airport next day to be shown round Concorde, which is a beautiful machine. We were also taken into the radar room and the control tower (a special privilege) and allowed to try on headphones, press buttons etc. This was all absolutely fascinating and very reassuring as none of us had realised that a flight really is monitored every inch of the way. We then all got on a plane and went off to Paris .....

More about the flight another time, but basically I feel I can now cope with flying, although it will never be my favourite activity!

Love,

Deborah

10 Did you find some of the speakers in this unit easier to understand than others? If you did, think about why that was. Was it due to:

- what the person was talking about?
- how fast they were talking?
- the kind of words they used?
- their accent?
- whether they were a man or a woman?
- how often they paused?

Are there any other factors which made the speakers more difficult or easier to understand?

Keep a note of the factors which make listening difficult for you and pay particular attention to them when you are doing listening practice.

Unit 3 Bumping Into People

Different people often see the same thing in different ways. In this unit you will hear people talking about a road accident that they either saw or were involved in. You will have to compare their statements.

On the 24th August 1986, at about midday, a car and a motorbike collided on a road in south London. Nobody was seriously injured, but detailed statements had to be made to the police (to decide if the law had been broken) and to insurance companies (to decide who was to pay for the damage).

1 Here is part of the statement that Mr J. McDonald, the car driver, made to the police. Copy the map below. Read Mr McDonald's statement, and mark on the map the positions and directions of the two vehicles at the time of the accident, and any other vehicles that were in the road at that time. Remember that, in Britain, people drive on the left.

14 In your opinion **who was to blame** for the accident?
Give your reasons briefly.

I hold the motorcyclist responsible for the accident. He was going much too fast. I had stopped at the junction of Terrapin Rd. and Bushnell Rd. and was just turning left into Bushnell Rd. There were lots of parked cars making Bushnell Rd. quite narrow. The motorcyclist suddenly appeared from the left. He must have been doing at least 40m.p.h. and was unable to stop before hitting me.

If you wish, draw a rough sketch in the space available below.

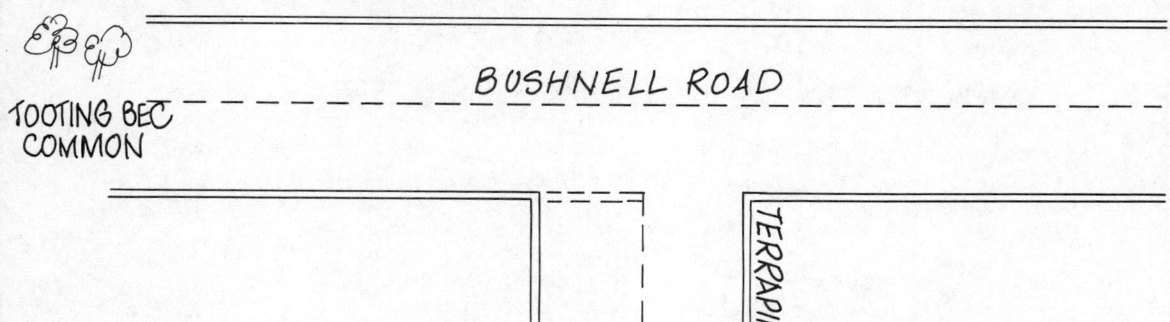

2 **a** Now listen to Mr D. Wilson, the motorcyclist, giving his account of the accident to a policeman. How is this account different from Mr McDonald's statement?

b Look at the form below, and note down what features of the driver the police would like a description of. Listen to the tape again, and write a description of Mr McDonald.

11. **Describe the driver** referred to in 8–10 above. *If possible, include sex, approximate age, height, build, complexion, colour of hair and eyes, and any other distinctive features.* Say whether you could recognise the driver again. State also whether the vehicle displayed 'L' plates and whether the driver was accompanied.

....

....

....

12. State whether you **recorded the registration mark** of a vehicle (give the mark) or whether this was recorded by someone else and passed to you. If the latter, give the name and address of the person who gave you the note. Say who has the note now and (if you have it) that you will be able to keep it safely and produce it at court if necessary.

3 A few weeks later, Miss Smith, of Terrapin Road, received the following letter:

SNATCH AND LEGGIT MOTOR INSURANCE CO.

Miss S. Smith
45 Terrapin Rd.
London SW 12

2nd Oct.1986

Dear Miss Smith,

Accident 24th August 1986
<u>Our Client: D.M. Wilson</u>

We understand that you were a witness to the above incident involving a car and a motorbike and we would appreciate it if you could assist us by forwarding a description of the accident.

We enclose a stamped addressed envelope and would thank you in anticipation.

Yours sincerely,

Snatch and Leggit

On the tape, Miss Smith is talking to a friend about the accident. Listen and take notes. (Miss Smith is the first person to speak.) Then copy the beginning of her reply to the insurance company below and complete it with the information you have got from the tape.

45 Terrapin Rd.,
London. SW12
7th Oct. 1986

Snatch and Leggit

Dear Sir/Madam,

With reference to the accident on 24th August 1986 involving your client, Mr. D.M. Wilson, to which I was a witness.

....

4 Form two groups. One group will be Snatch and Leggit, the other McKillet and Skinnet Ins. Co. (representing Mr McDonald). Talk together and reach an agreement on who will pay for the damage to the vehicles.

SWINDLE GARAGE

Front nearside wheel arch	40
Labour	65
	£105

POCKETT
MOTORCYCLE SERVICES

Front headlamp unit	52
Front wheel	24
Labour	30
	£106

5 Miss Smith and her friend use the following verbs when they are talking about the accident (task 3):

knock down **turn into**
knock off **pull out of**

Use these verbs to describe what is happening in the two pictures at the top of the next page. If you are not sure what the words mean, listen to the tape again first.

6 In the conversation you heard in task 3, Miss Smith and her friend talk about what they think happened, and they make suppositions about things they are not sure about.

For example: '*Perhaps* he was tired.'

Listen to their conversation again and write down all the expressions they use to make suppositions or to express uncertainty.

7 Look at the picture below and talk about what you think has happened. Use some of the expressions you have just noted down.

Think about:
- where the road is.
- how the bus got where it is.
- how fast it was going.
- what happened to the driver and the passengers.

Unit 4 Learning How: Learning? How?

This unit is about why people learn foreign languages and how they go about it. You will hear English-speaking people talking about their experiences of learning different languages, and will be asked to think about how you learn English.

1 Why, according to the following extract from the publication *Executive Post*, is it important to learn foreign languages?

WITH more than half of Britain's overseas trade now going to continental Europe, and barely a quarter to English-speaking markets in the USA and Commonwealth, no one involved in export marketing and sales can afford to be complacent about weak or non-existent foreign language skills.

The importance of foreign languages for overseas trade has been documented in a number of studies over the years. The most frequently cited of these, the British Overseas Trade Board report, published in 1979, stressed that there was in many cases a clear need for exporters to use a foreign language – 50 per cent of German and Austrian firms, for instance, requiring correspondence in German. Many British companies were found to rely heavily on the language skills of their agents, leading to a lack of in-depth market intelligence and customer contact. Yet at the same time, according to another report, produced by the British Export Trade Research Association, nearly 40 per cent of British export directors and 60 per cent of export salesmen had no significant language ability.

2 Talk to as many other people in the class as you can and find out why each person is studying English. Ask questions to find as many reasons as possible, and make a list.

3 Listen to these five people talking about why they studied different languages. Which of the languages mentioned in the article at the top of the next page did they study and why? Are any of their reasons on the list you made for task 2?

The people you are going to hear are:

1 Donald
2 Simon
3 Brenda
4 Peter
5 Richard

Which languages?

Reeves and Liston's findings indicate that the languages which are most useful for careers in overseas trade are French and German, with German perhaps having a slight edge. This view is borne out by a recent survey, *Foreign Language Use in Northern Industry and Commerce*, carried out by Stephen Hagen of Newcastle upon Tyne Polytechnic. He asked over 200 companies whether they felt there were any countries or regions where they could have significantly improved their trade performance with access to foreign languages. A majority of the respondents said that there were, and when asked to specify the particular languages that would have been useful, came up with the following league table:

German (mentioned by 51 per cent of companies);
French (48 per cent);
Spanish (27.5 per cent);
Arabic (25 per cent);
Italian (15.5 per cent);
Japanese (9 per cent);
Russian (5 per cent);
Chinese (4.5 per cent).

The interest in Japanese probably reflects the siting of Nissan in the region, but otherwise the results, particularly as far as the top five languages are concerned, are probably indicative of the nationwide picture.

4 The article below is about foreign language learning in British schools. In what ways in this situation different from the learning of English in schools in your country?

Language failure starts in school

ONLY about one-third of those who begin a foreign language course complete more than three years' study, and at the age of 13 few can speak fluently and grammatically or produce coherent and accurate writing of any length, says a recent report from the Department of Education and Science.

The report contains the results of a survey commissioned by the DES from the National Foundation for Educational Research. It covers pupils studying French in schools in England, Wales and Northern Ireland, and German and Spanish in English schools alone.

Other findings include the suggestions that girls perform better than boys, although the gap is narrower in French than in German and Spanish, and that children are inhibited by preoccupation with correctness.

• *Foreign Language Performance in Schools: Report on the 1983 Survey of French, German and Spanish is available (while stocks last) from the DES Assessment of Performance Unit, Elizabeth House, York Road, London SE1 7PH.*

5 Listen to David and Muriel. Why do they think the English do not speak foreign languages well?

6 **a** Listen to these people talking about the problems they have had learning different languages. Listen and make a note of the problems.

b Are any of these problems similar to ones that you have had with English? Compare your experience with what the people on the tape said and make a list of all the language learning problems you can think of. Then try to find ways of overcoming them.

7 Here are extracts from answers that two different trainee teachers wrote in their final examination in response to the question, 'Discuss the role of the teacher in the English language class'. They represent unusually extreme views. Which one do you agree with more? Why?

I see my role as a teacher as one of informant (I know the language), director (I am the teacher) and conductor (I know what the students have to do in order to learn). So I have to prepare my classes well by deciding what the students will learn and how. Therefore, one of the most important tasks is to convince the students to learn in the way that I want them to.

1

....and this is indeed a far from simple question.

I realise that every student is different and learns in a very individual way. It is therefore impossible to provide a set of teaching or learning procedures that will suit everyone in the class. I feel then, that one of my main functions as a teacher is, apart from 'giving' the students the language, to help them to become better, more efficient learners. By this, I mean learners who are more independent, more self-directed and more able to choose the learning style - techniques and materials - that suits them best.

In order to do this, I expect to introduce the students to a variety of learning techniques and materials in order to help them evaluate these for themselves and gradually to move towards a class where students themselves decide what they want or need and how they are going to achieve it.

2

8 **a** Listen to these people talking about the strategies they have used to learn different languages, and make notes.

The people are:

1 Roger
2 Simon
3 Brenda
4 Ravi

b Have you used any of the same strategies? Did they work? Have you used any others?

Make a list of all the strategies you know, say whether you find them useful or not, and give your reasons. This chart might help you.

The student has to come to grips with different elements and aspects of the language. For example:

Language Skills

Listening Speaking Reading Writing

Components of Language

Pronunciation Grammar Vocabulary

There is also the question of fluency and accuracy, the ability to speak naturally and correctly.

Unit 5 The Cassette Letter

John Greenland is an English language teacher. He has worked in Britain, Canada and Sweden.

Recently, he accepted a post in Malaysia, in a tiny village called Batu Rakit, on the east coast of the Malaysian Peninsula near Kuala Terengganu. While living in Canada, John started sending taped messages to his parents instead of letters. It was cheaper than using the telephone and he found he could say much more than he could in a letter.

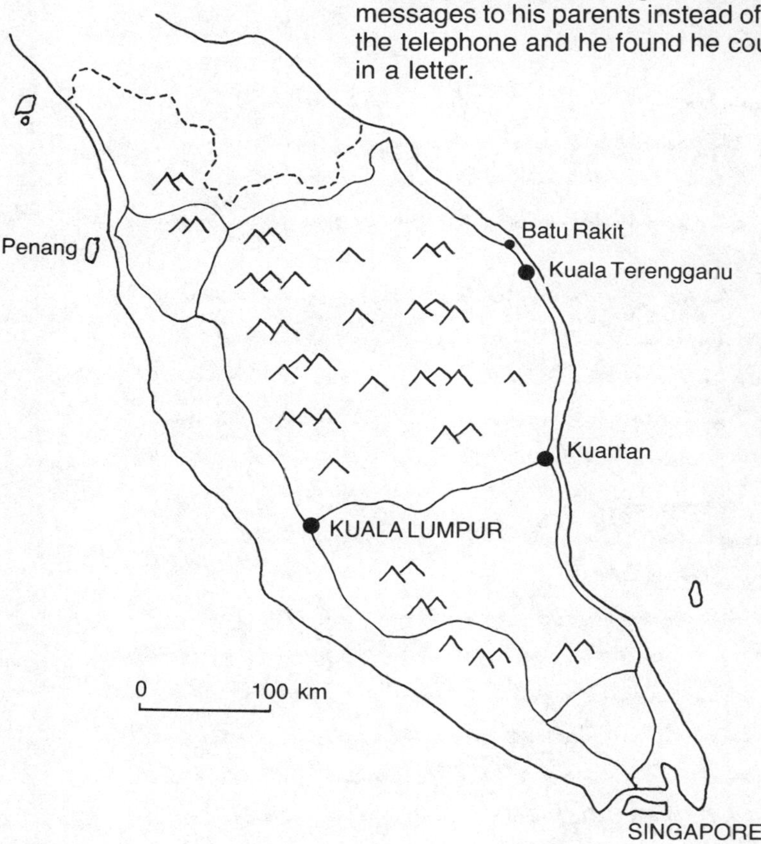

1 Read the questions below, and then listen to this part of the first tape that John sent his parents from Malaysia.

a How did John find his house?

b Who helped him?

c What did he think of the house at first?

d There is something most unusual about this house. What is it?

e How much does he pay for it?

2 A few weeks later, John received this letter from his parents. Read the questions below. Then read the letter and answer the questions.

a Where do they live?

b Where have they been recently? Why?

c Who do you think Richard and Caroline are?

Taunton
Sunday 21st Nov.

Dear John,

Thanks for your tape - your new life sounds very different. We're glad you had time to relax a little in Kuala Lumpur when you arrived. Your description of all the different foods sounds marvellous.

We hope you're settling into your new house now - especially that you've got some chairs. What is "rattan" exactly, by the way? Imagine you've bought yourself a bicycle by now. What are the roads like? And don't go rushing into buying a car - it's best to wait awhile. Remember the trouble you had with that old Fiat you bought?

Well, enough of questions about you. I expect you received our postcard from Lynmouth. We decided to have a short break before the winter sets in. In fact it was dry and cold with some sun, and there was a little snow on the tops of the hills. A lot different from your weather! We stayed in a very comfortable Bed and Breakfast and had some lovely walks.

Richard's moved into his new flat. He's very lucky. We've given him the old wardrobe from the back bedroom, and the ancient sofa. When he's settled in he should be very comfortable. He's coming down next weekend. Caroline probably will too. She rang last night. She was very excited as she's just heard that she's passed all her secretarial exams with flying colours. So I expect we'll have a bit of a celebration.

That's most of the news from us. We all think of you, and picture you in your wooden house. We felt sorry for you, sitting alone in the darkness when you had the power cut! Careful what you eat, and don't forget to boil the well-water!

Much love,

Mum and Dad

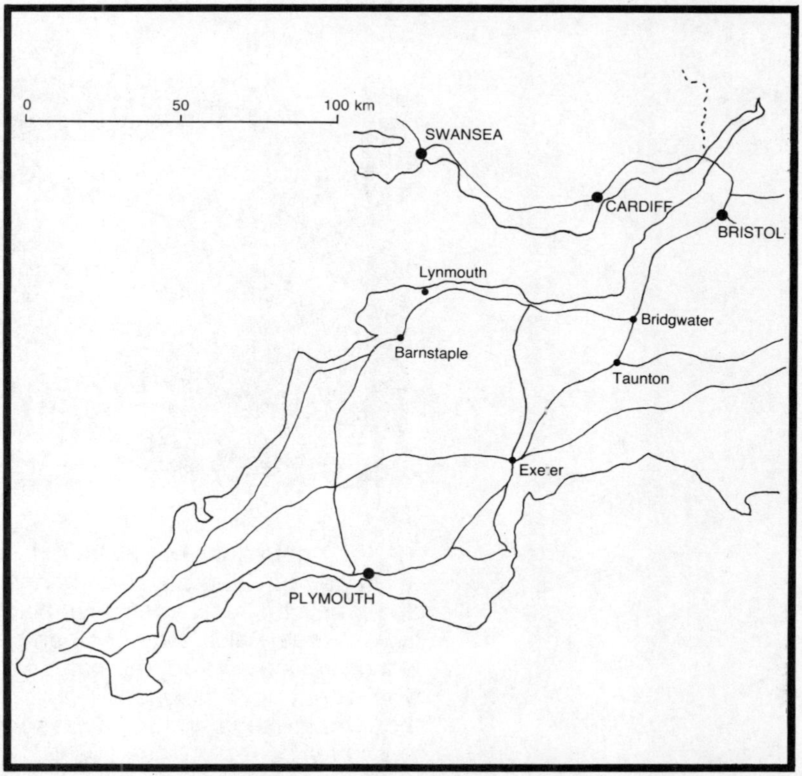

3 You have heard only part of John's first cassette letter to his parents. Read again the letter sent to John by his parents in reply to this first cassette. From what they say in their letter, what else must he have talked about on the rest of the cassette?

4 On a later cassette letter, made after John had settled in, he tried to describe the atmosphere of his new house.

a Listen to John talking about some of his 'evening visitors'. Before you listen, read the following questions, and try to answer them as you listen.

- Which visitors does he like? Why?
- Which visitors does he not like? Why?
- Which visitors don't really bother him?

b Now listen as he describes three night noises. What makes them?

5 The following month, John's father wrote to say that they had not had any news since the first cassette letter in October. John realised that the second cassette must have been delayed in the post, so he quickly sent off an airmail letter. From what you can remember of the contents of the second tape (task 4), write a letter to John's father.

6 John's house in Malaysia is very different from his parents' house in England which you can see below. How many differences can you make out? Can you explain the differences (climate, building materials, economy, etc.)?

7 Why not send a cassette letter yourself? Instead of writing to a pen pal, you could exchange cassette letters with someone and practise speaking and listening in English. Find an organisation in your area which arranges pen pals or ask at your local British Council office and get the names and addresses of some people who want to correspond in English. Then write to them and ask if they would like to exchange cassette letters. You could do this either individually or as a class.

If you only want to practise listening to English, rather than speaking it, you could contact English-speaking people who are studying your language: then you could send cassettes in your language while they reply in English.

Unit 6 A Fit Of Keeping Fit

This unit is about physical exercise and keeping fit. You will hear people talking about the kinds of exercise they take and why, and you will be able to talk about the sports and exercises that you do.

1 Why does the writer of this text think we should take exercise?

Living in a caveman body

Illustration by Ken Taylor

MAYBE you feel great as you are. Full of beans. Always on the go. Maybe you look pretty healthy too. Sparkling eyes, plenty of colour in your cheeks.

So why bother to exercise? If you're fit enough to drive a car, use a washing machine, work the motor mower or the electric drill, that's all that matters, isn't it?

Far from it.

Although you inhabit an electronic, push-button, high-technology world, you still have a Stone Age body. It took millions of years of evolution for the human body to become adapted for primitive survival – for running, fighting, jumping, lifting, dragging, climbing – in order to hunt, trap and gather food. It simply hasn't had time to adapt to our modern mollycoddled way of life.

Your body was designed for vigorous daily activity. And it misses it.

2 Do you agree with the above writer? What form of exercise do you take? Talk to other people in the class and find out about them.

3 Listen to the people on the tape talking about the forms of exercise they take and make a list of the different types. Compare their reasons for doing exercise with the ones given in the list below and note down any that are not in the list.

The people you are going to hear are:

1 Alison	4 Iain
2 Susanna	5 Bridget
3 Tim	6 Deborah

Benefits and bonuses

* Exercise improves the staying power of your heart and circulation and may protect against coronary heart disease.
* It keeps your neck, back and joints supple and your posture right.
* It tightens flabby muscles and gives you strength.
* It helps you stay slim.
* It helps to combat stress.
* It can be great fun.
* And it helps you feel good, in mind as well as body.

4 The writer of the text below divides forms of exercise into two types. Read the text, then listen to the tape again and classify, according to what the writer says, the forms of exercise that the people on the tape mention.

BASICALLY, exercise is either 'static' or 'dynamic' depending on whether or not it produces movement. In **static** exercises (sometimes called 'isometrics'), muscles contract against resistance without any movement of the limbs, as in tug-of-war.

Although good for body-building, **static** exercises aren't much good for increasing heart and lung efficiency, which means that on their own they're *not* enough to get you fit. What's more, they can cause sudden peaks of high blood pressure – potentially harmful in the middle-aged.

In **dynamic** exercises the limbs are moved rhythmically. The larger the muscles and the more vigorous the effort, the greater the demand for oxygen in the blood – and the better the exercise is for heart and lungs. So, for real fitness, activities involving dynamic exercise of the legs are most effective.

5 The text at the top of the next page, about jogging, comes from a publicity leaflet produced to encourage people to take up doing exercise. Use it as a model to write a similar text about one of the forms of exercise mentioned on the tape. Do not forget to:

- say what it does for your body.
- say what the form of exercise consists of.
- say something to encourage people to take it up.

1. Say what it does for your body.

2 Say what it consists of.

The gentle jog to fitness

JOGGING not only makes you feel great, it is also one of the most natural and effective ways of exercising the heart and lungs. Jogging is running free and easy, at a comfortable trot. There's no urgency, no strain, no competition.

The idea is to jog along at a pace that makes you no more than moderately breathless. If you do it for long enough and often enough, in gradually increasing sessions (see below), it will soon build up the stamina of your heart and lungs, and strengthen your leg muscles. And the steady, easy rhythm of jogging will help to massage away mental and physical tension and lift depression. The joy of jogging is that virtually anyone can do it, young or old. You can do it, anywhere or anytime.

3. Expand on 1 and 2.

4. Encourage people to take it up.

6 **a** Read this text and write a word to fill each of the blanks. In some cases, more than one word is possible. Choose the one you think most appropriate.

STAMINA BUILDER that's easy on the feet

Cycling is not only a ______1______ way to keep ______2______, but also it's free, it's ______3______ and it's faster than ______4______. Forget all that Tour de France stuff. You can cycle as speedily or as ______5______ as you like.

It ______6______ the strength of your legs and helps to keep them mobile. It is also an excellent way to ______7______ up stamina of heart and ______8______, providing you ______9______ hard enough, for long ______10______. And, ______11______ jogging, it has the great advantage that you don't have to bear your ______12______ on your feet, so it's much ______13______ for people with painful feet or arthritis.

b What information did you use to choose the words? Did you make use of any of the following?

- Knowledge of grammar.
- Knowledge of what part of speech was needed: verb, noun, etc.
- Words that you learned in this unit.
- 'Good guessing'.
- Familiarity with the topic.
- Deduction.

Did you use anything else? Make a list of all the things you used.

Now try to put the list in order of importance. Does this tell you anything about how you use and learn a language?

Unit 7 Building Buildings

The Pompidou Centre in Paris was designed by the British architect Richard Rogers and his Italian partner Renzo Piano together with international engineers and German steelmakers.

1 You are going to hear some people talking about the Pompidou Centre. Make notes on the information they give about the building and what they feel about it.

The people are:

1 Elizabeth and Mike
2 Peter and Deborah
3 Chuck

2 If you can, work in small groups. Find out if anyone in your group has ever visited the Pompidou Centre and, if so, what they thought of it. Decide whether you would like to see something similar in your town or city.

3 In 1980, work began on the new Lloyd's building in the City of London. Lloyd's is a large and expanding insurance market, and it chose Richard Rogers as the architect for its new building. Read the following articles. Why did Lloyd's choose Richard Rogers?

The great advantage of Richard Rogers' design is that the size of the Room can be varied with relative ease and the galleries opening onto the central atrium will ensure that the atmosphere of a single market is retained.

The building is also capable of handling the high population densities which are associated with the Lloyd's market—lifts, escalators, lavatories and staircases being designed to meet more effectively than at present the demands of a significantly larger market.

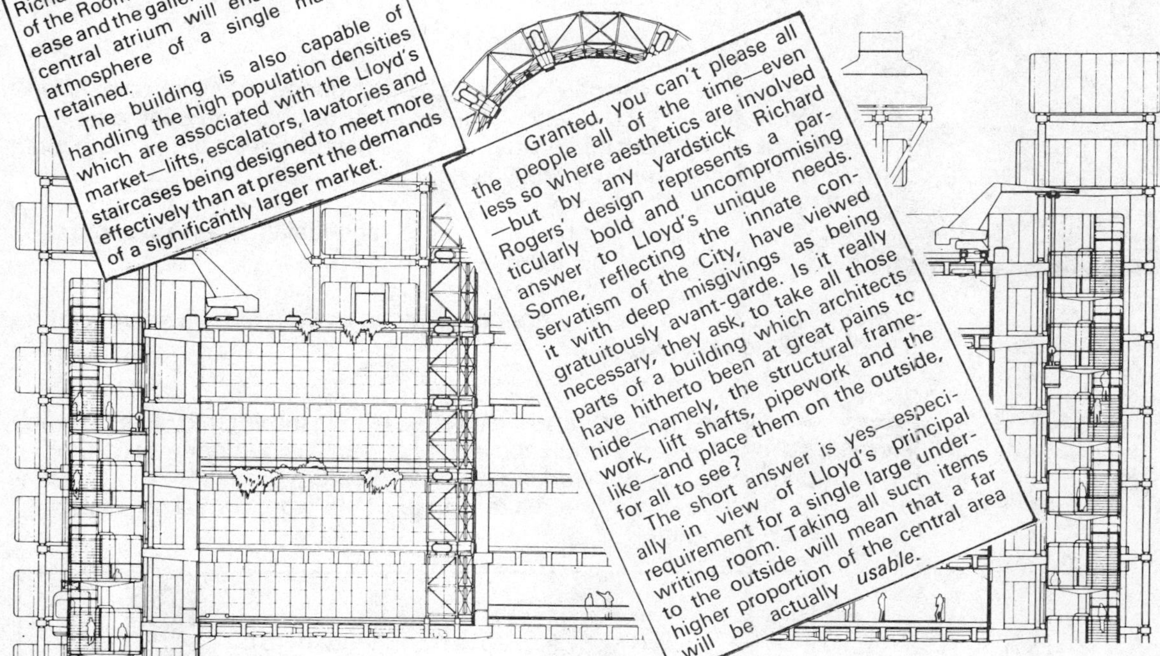

Granted, you can't please all the people all of the time—even less so where aesthetics are involved—but by any yardstick Richard Rogers' design represents a particularly bold and uncompromising answer to Lloyd's unique needs. Some, reflecting the innate conservatism of the City, have viewed it with deep misgivings as being gratuitously avant-garde. Is it really necessary, they ask, to take all those parts of a building which architects have hitherto been at great pains to hide—namely, the structural framework, lift shafts, pipework and the like—and place them on the outside, for all to see?

The short answer is yes—especially in view of Lloyd's principal requirement for a single large underwriting room. Taking all such items to the outside will mean that a far higher proportion of the central area will be actually *usable*.

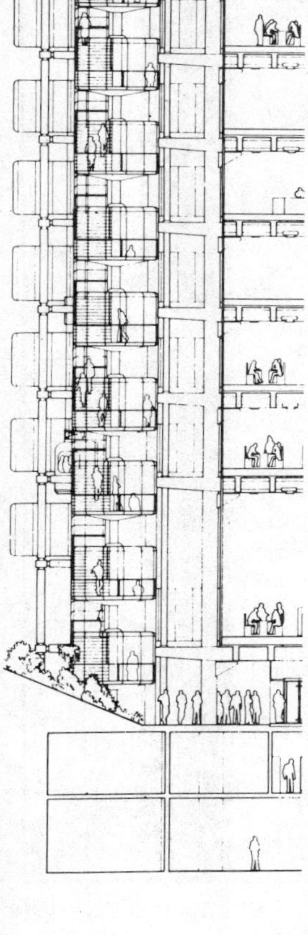

4 Now listen to Philip explaining why the Richard Rogers design was chosen for the Paris arts centre. What features do the Pompidou Centre and the Lloyd's building have in common?

5 Read this extract from *The Ice Age* by Margaret Drabble. Len Wincobank, a property developer, is thinking. Do you agree with his thoughts?

> England. What was the matter with it? Shabby, lazy, unambitious, complacently high-minded when it so chose.
>
> He thought of America. New York, the most beautiful city in the world, the apotheosis of aspiration. What buildings there, what inspiration, what vision, what glory, steel, glass, concrete, Art Nouveau, Art Deco, brutality, fountains, spires, windows, avenues, intersections, passion and desire. Or Chicago, with the glittering lake front, the water that flowed backwards, the highest building in the world, the largest multi-coloured fountain in the world, a paradise of invention and felicity. They said that Sydney was beautiful too. When he got out, he would go and have a look at Sydney, and pick up a few ideas.

Unit 8 The Dictaphone

Molly Keaveney runs a small nursing agency in Dublin called *Erin Recruitment*. The agency recruits staff for hospitals overseas, particularly the Middle East. It is a small business but it has been very successful and Molly is kept busy.

When Molly cannot be in the office, she leaves messages and instructions on a dictaphone for her secretary.

1 Listen to the tape and make notes of what Molly's secretary has to do today.

2 When the secretary has finished writing the letter to Miss O'Brien, she makes a photocopy of it for her files. Unfortunately, the photocopier is not working properly. Look at the letter below, listen to the tape again and make a note of the words which are missing from the letter.

ERI[redacted]cruitment, 43 Fitzroy St.,
[redacted]lin 2 Tel. 334666

14th April [redacted]

Miss J. O'Br[redacted]
Parade Walk [redacted]
Dublin

Dear Miss O[redacted]

We are pleas[redacted]make you an offer of employment[redacted]CO Clinic, Jedd[redacted]copy of the contract is enclose[redacted]we have your ac[redacted]ce in writing as soon as possib[redacted]

This offer i[redacted]ect to a satisfactory medical e[redacted]ion. Would you [redacted] telephone our office to a[redacted] an appointment [redacted]ur medical officer? You will al[redacted] to bring your p[redacted]t, ten passport-sized photograp[redacted]the originals of[redacted]nursing certificates.

We look forw[redacted] hearing from you.

Yours sincer[redacted]

Molly Keaven[redacted]

3 Write a letter to Joan Ryan, telling her that she did not get the job in Jeddah.

4 Here is the advertisement that appeared in the *Nursing Weekly*. Read it carefully and:

- decide what is wrong with it. (Listen to the tape again if necessary.)
- make sure you understand all the words and expressions.

)R
SA

ficate or
you.

tandards
medical

ıtact:

(5680)L

ERIN
RECRUITMENT
CHARGE NURSE I.C.U. KUWAIT

Six years' post registration experience
with some experience in ward control.

Benefits include:
- Excellent tax-free salary
- Free furnished accommodation
- Free air fares
- Generous leave allowance
- Free medical cover

Applications, enclosing full c.v. to:
ERIN Recruitment (ref. KWT/ICU)
43 Fitzroy St., Dublin 2
Tel: 334626

SA
We h
NUR
MIDV
at 1
Sauc
For r
tele

NU
Fc
Sund

South Australia
The Queen Elizabeth Hospital
IURSE EDUCATORS

:ations are invited from qualified Nurse Educators
sh to migrate to Australia.
rse Educators should have a minimum of two
nical experience and a proven high level of
d ability in clinical and classroom teaching. A
Teaching (Nurse Education) or its equivalent
sful applicants will work with a
lement educational programmes
al practice within the School of

can be

vs

Mount Elizabeth Hospita
Singapore
DIRECTOR O
NURSING

National Medical Enterprises Inc, one of the le
international health-care companies in the
and manages the prestigious private Mo
Hospital in Singapore.

This 485 bed facility offers a wide ranc
speciality services including cardiothc
renal transplantation.

We are seeking an enthusiastic ind
communication skills who can d
administrative ability, but
knowledge to maintain

The succ
prefe

5 Using the advertisement in task 4 as an example, write out the advertisement for the dental nurse which Molly wants her secretary to place. First look at the advertisement in task 4 and note down the points of information which you think you will need. Then listen to the tape again for the information.

6 When you call Jim, the plumber, you hear this recorded message. What do you say?

7 Work in pairs, learner A and learner B. Look at your task sheet. It has half of a letter of application for the job advertised in the *Nursing Weekly*; your partner has the other half. The objective of this task is for both of you to dictate your half of the letter to the other so that you both end up with the complete letter. Follow this procedure when dictating:

a First read through your half of the letter and divide it up into the phrases that you can dictate comfortably. E.g.

|*Please reply as soon as you can,*|*confirming your acceptance.*|

b Then dictate in the following way. Read a phrase silenty, then look up from the page at your partner and say it. If you find you cannot remember it, read it again silently and look up again and say it. Learner A begins and dictates the first section on his/her task sheet, then learner B continues with the first section on his/her task sheet. Then learner A reads his/her second section and so on until the letter is complete.

c Finally, check the dictation by looking at your partner's task sheet.

TASK SHEET A

4 Meadows Lane
Dublin 18
17th April 1987

[redacted]

Dear Ms Keaveney

<u>Your reference KWT/ICU</u>

[redacted] As you can see from my cv (enclosed) I have had fifteen years' nursing experience, five of which were spent abroad, in Africa and the Far East.

[redacted]

I am about to take a short holiday in France but I would be available to attend an interview any time after the end of next week.

[redacted]

Thank you for your attention. I look forward to hearing from you soon.

[redacted]

[redacted]

TASK SHEET B

[redacted]

Erin Recruitment
43 Fitzroy St
Dublin 2

[redacted]

[redacted]

I am writing in response to your advertisement in the Nursing Weekly, inviting applications for the post of Charge Nurse in Kuwait. [redacted]

I have just completed a two year contract in Malaysia and would be very interested in taking up another appointment overseas.

[redacted]

If you decide to take up references, please do not hesitate to contact any of those that I have listed on my cv.

[redacted]

Yours sincerely

Penny Crossland

Unit 9 Character Sketches

This unit is about Roger, who lives and works in London. You will hear some of his friends talking about him and you will think about different aspects of his life, such as his house or his handwriting, that express aspects of his personality.

1 Listen to Fiona talking about Roger and decide which of the three options in each question below best describes him.

a i extrovert
ii introvert
iii neither

b i defeatist
ii determined
iii neither

c i caring
ii superficial
iii neither

d i slow
ii sharp
iii neither

e i a calming influence
ii hyperactive
iii neither

f i a listener
ii a doer
iii neither

2 Which of the following photographs do you think is of Roger? Why?

1

2

3

4

3 **a** Read this article, and then, in pairs or groups, decide which of the three examples of handwriting is Roger's.

Graphology actually works out perfectly for any kind of handwriting, be it in Arabic, Russian, Gothic-German or English. After understanding how a child learns to write in school, the analyst studies the script under a magnifying glass. (Prior knowledge of age and gender are useful, however). How does the graphologist arrive at his conclusions? Researchers during the past 400 years discovered certain similarities in the scripts of honest (or dishonest), modest (or conceited), intelligent (or stupid) people, among many other categories.

Slightly oversimplified, here's how graphology works: strong strokes denote a strong person; the strength may be moral or physical. An erratic, undisciplined individual will write in an erratic, undisciplined way. A man who has a great sense of order in all phases of life, including business, will write in an orderly fashion. While the above may sound like generalizations, these and dozens of other rules apply to every handwriting, and serve here merely as examples.

This slant shows that the writer who prefers the 90° stance instead of a right or left slant is usually a self-controlled individual

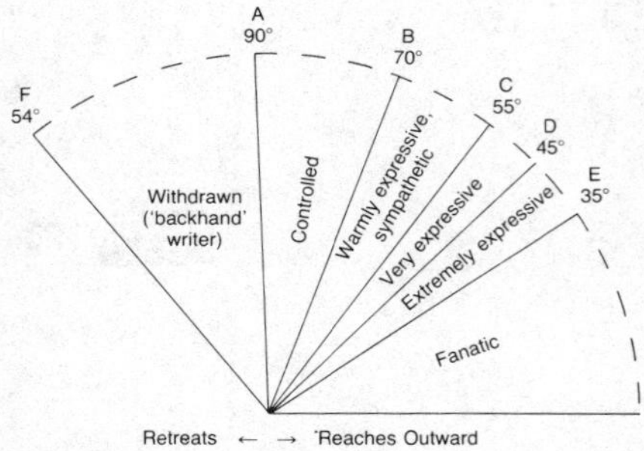

1

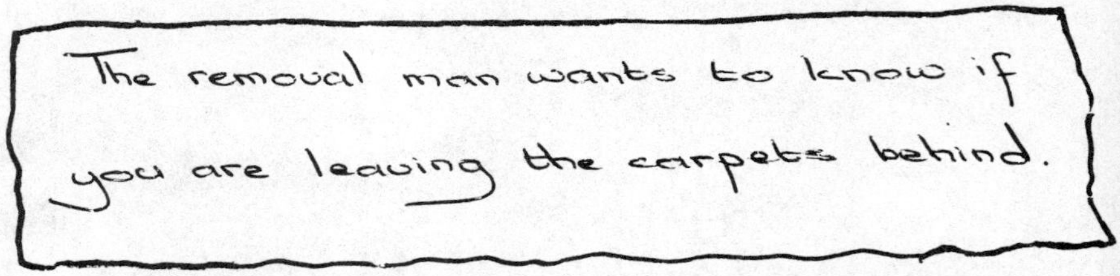

2

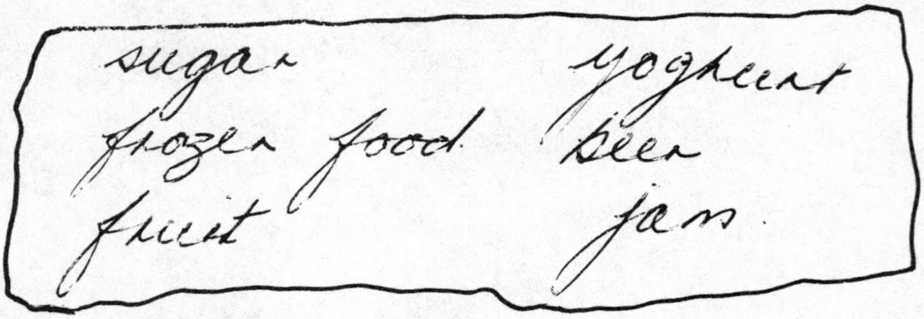

3

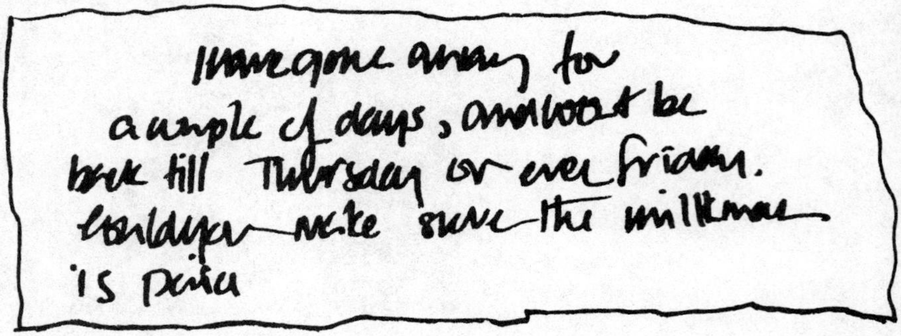

b Now work in pairs. Give each other a sample of your own handwriting and use the information in the texts opposite to analyse your partner's personality. When you have finished, tell your partner what you have found, and check whether he or she agrees or not.

4 **a** Listen to Dave describing two very different sitting-rooms. Decide which one is Roger's. Give reasons for your answers.

b Can you think of any other things that reflect a person's personality? Make a list.

5 Prepare a character description of somebody known to the whole class (a student, a teacher, a famous person). You should include information about handwriting, clothes, taste in music, etc. but *not* about physical appearance. Do not give the name of the person.

When you have finished, EITHER read your description out loud OR display what you have written on the noticeboard or on the wall, and let the other learners guess whom you chose to describe.

6 If you can, work in small groups. Choose someone known to the class and imagine them as different things (e.g. a colour, a tree, a car, something to eat). Make a list and report back like this:

If this person were a colour, this person would be red.

The rest of the class will have to guess who the person is. NB. Do not say a colour just because the person is wearing it today, or a car just because the person owns one at the moment.

7 What kind of learning personality have you got? Look at the following questions. Discuss with some other learners your answers and what they say about your learning personality.

1 Does it bother you if you make mistakes?
2 Do you enjoy working in pairs and groups?
3 Do you want to listen to and talk to the other learners in the class as well as to the teacher?
4 Do you ask questions if you do not understand?
5 Do you ask the other learners for help before asking the teacher?
6 Do you expect to learn all your English in the classroom?
7 Do you know what you do well in English and what you do badly?
8 When you listen, are you worried if you do not understand every word?
9 When you speak, do you think more about what you want to say or how you are going to say it?
10 Do you use English books and dictionaries a lot outside the classroom?

Unit 10 Melody Maker

In this unit you will listen to different people talking about music and why they like it. You will also hear them playing some pieces of music that they like and will be able to compare your opinions with theirs.

1 Which word is the 'odd man out' in each of these lists? What do the three others in each list have in common?

1	2	3	4	5
note	song	choir	voice	play
score	harmony	orchestra	wind	hum
rhythm	tune	duet	string	sing
beat	melody	band	percussion	practise

2 Listen to these people talking about why they like producing music, and answer these questions.

a What instrument do they each play?

b What are the pleasures they get from music?

The people you will hear are:

1 David Poole
2 Annie (talking to David Mann)
3 David Mann (talking to Annie)

3 Do you produce music or do you listen to music? What kind of music do you like and why?

Find out about some of the other people in the class.

4 David Poole, and David Mann and Annie, recorded some of their music on our tape and talked about why they like the particular pieces they recorded. Listen to them talking and:

a make a note of why they like the piece they are going to play;

b try to write down all the adjectives they use to describe the music.

5 Now listen to the music and give your own opinion.

6 Read this review of a new record and make a note of all the adjectives used. Are any of them the same as those you noted down for task 4, or do any of them mean the same thing? Classify the adjectives according to whether they are positive (+) or negative (−).

Reissues from 1962, '64

Heard immediately after Philips' Tate/U… concertos the sound is electrifyingly good, a model of what CD can do for recordings of such vintage, and a restorative of one's hope for technology. Clear definition, excellent balance, and vital, sparkling performances from Davis/LSO, and silky-smooth fiddling from a master of sensuous sound. **[A:1/1*]**

Kenneth Dommett

MOZART: Violin Concertos K216 & K219 **[CD]**
Kim Sjögren (vln)/Collegium Musicum Copenhagen/Schonwandt
BIS CD-282 (58m 11s) (LP: BIS LP-282, NMC)

The Holte Gymnasium, Copenhagen, has imparted a full-bodied and resonant sound to this small-scale Mozart and may account for the explosive *szforzandos* at the beginning of K216, which are alarming and rather ugly. Both music and recording quickly settle into a more stylish pattern though, and Sjögren's playing is a source of much pleasure. He has a fine tone and a firm touch allied to a good understanding of the demands of the music, its combination of lyricism and strength. The two slow movements are particularly attractive. The little Copenhagen orchestra has polish but is not over-refined, and its young conductor (once a student at the RCM) has a real feeling for Mozart. **[A:1]** **Kenneth Dommett**

MOZART: Sinfonia Concertante K364 □ **[LP]**
Violin Concerto K216
Sir Yehudi Menuhin (vln)/Luigi Bianchi (vla)/ECO/ Menuhin
EMI EG 27 02361 digital dmm (NCD, MC: EG 27 02364)

28…
Christia…
EMI EL 27…

The second … well up to the … '85 p125). Here … power of the … judiciously. His … crystalline in its c… the beginning of K… delicate yet emphatic… appears far removed f… da's; slow movements … but there is no dwelling o… instance, his reading of … K333 demonstrates. Notwit… are fine and searching per… piano sound is a little on the … than concert setting wo… reasonable enough in a d… **[A:1]**

MOZART: Requiem
Kathleen Battle/Ann M… Salminen/Orch & Ch d…
EMI CDC 7 473422 (5… 01941, MC: EL 27 019…

The LP (Oct '85 p11… in all departments, … scholarly. The C… improve on the LP; … parameters and the … after all though. **[A:…**

MOZART: Requi…
Cotrubas/Watt…

7 Use the review above as a model to write a review of a record you know or have heard recently.

Unit 11 Read All About It!

Have you ever noticed that the same news item is often reported in different ways in different newspapers? Or that it often sounds different if read in the newspaper and heard on the radio? In this unit you will read the news in different newspapers and listen to a radio broadcast reporting the same stories.

1 Look at these headlines from *The Times* newspaper of the 21st May 1986. What do you think the articles are about?

1 **Hijack over**

2 **Hurd gives go-ahead for police to increase manpower by 3,200**

3 **New jobs fury as BR sheds another 5,900**

4 **Firemen free boy from shaft**

5 **Angry Thatcher still rules out sanctions**

6 **Lorry kills three schoolgirls**

7 **£25m art theft at Irish mansion**

2 Now listen to a news bulletin, broadcast on the radio on the same day. Did the radio give the same news items as *The Times*? Match the headlines with the news items on the radio and check whether you predicted the topics correctly. Do not worry about detail, and remember that the radio may not report all the items that the newspaper reported.

3 Look at these headlines from other newspapers reporting some of the same news items. How are some of them different from the headlines above? What do they tell you about the different newspapers which are published? Which are from 'popular', and which from 'quality', papers?

1 **Diggers rescue boy from shaft**

2 **Maggie: No sanctions for raids**

3 **SAVED!**
Tunnel trap boy comes up smiling

4 **ARTFUL DODGE OF £30m RAIDERS**

5 **BR strike threat at 'savage' job cuts**

4 Look at these articles about two of the news items and listen again to them being reported on the radio. (They are the last two items in the broadcast you listened to for task 2.) Make a note of any differences between what is reported in the newspaper and what the radio says.

2

Diggers rescue boy from shaft

A boy who was trapped by his legs after falling down a ventilation shaft was dug out by three industrial earthmovers yesterday.

Benjamin Crouch, aged nine, fell 14 feet down the 15 inch wide hole set in the side of a grassy bank at Dover Castle, Kent. The earthmovers cut into the side of the bank and then firemen hacked through the side of the brick-lined tunnel.

It took the rescuers three hours to reach Benjamin, of Old Road, East Peckham, Kent. He was suffering from shock and bruising.

The shaft was inspected by castle staff just a few hours earlier and they had decided to cover it permanently as it was considered dangerous. The acting head custodian, Mrs Patricia Scott, said: "Obviously we are sorry this little lad fell down the hole, but he should never have been on this bank."

Benjamin was one of a party of children from St George's Special School, in Tunbridge Wells, Kent, visiting the castle.

1

Thieves take £10m paintings in Irish raid

From Joe Joyce in Dublin

IRISH police were last night awaiting a ransom demand for the safe return of paintings valued at up to £10 million, which were taken from the home of Sir Alfred Beit early yesterday.

Seventeen works of art, including one of Vermeer's best-known paintings, were seized from Russborough House, County Wicklow, for the second time in 12 years.

Seven of the less valuable works were found abandoned alongside a jeep several miles away. Two were badly damaged.

An alarm at the house went off in the local police station at 2 am yesterday and a patrol went to the mansion, where they alerted the curator, Michael O'Shea. He checked every room, but all appeared to be normal.

The robbery was discovered six hours later when Colonel O'Shea returned to open the building. Detectives believe the gang triggered the alarm and moved in after the police had left.

They drove two vehicles across fields to the back of the house and broke in through a window without setting off the alarms again. They took the paintings, still in their frames, from three rooms.

5 Newspaper headlines are shorter and more contracted than the news headlines given on the radio. Look at these newspaper headlines. Then listen to the tape and write down the corresponding radio news headlines.

1 **Man charged with stabbing**

2 **Oxfordshire to get 1½m**

3 **Youth worker sentenced**

4 **Angry Thatcher still rules out sanctions**

5 **Hurd gives go-ahead for police to increase manpower by 3,200**

6 **New jobs fury as BR sheds another 5,900**

6 Now write radio news headlines for these newspaper headlines:

1 **Sanctions row may split Commonwealth**

2 **No clue to paintings stolen in Irish robbery**

3 **Mass job losses warning**

4 **Police tear gas rioting whites**

5 **Zimbabwe holds two whites after Pretoria's attack**

7 If you do not live in an English-speaking country and you want more listening practice, why not listen to BBC English by Radio lessons? There are regular broadcasts which can be picked up in most countries at different times of the day. These include a wide selection of programmes. Here is some information to help you pick up the broadcasts. Read the texts below and opposite and answer the following questions.

a If a programme is timed at 2245 GMT, what time will it be broadcast in Greece?

b Which two programmes advertised interest you most?

c On what wave bands would you be able to pick up the programmes if you lived in the USSR?

	For programme times see section under map	At 12.45 and 21.30
SATURDAY	**SILENT CONVERSATION** — Listening comprehension based on monologues. 1.11.86 POP WORDS — Series explaining the lyrics of pop songs. 31.1.87 TAKING OFF — low level course following the lives of a rich air company family. (support material available).	**SPY IN THE SKY** — intermediate thriller serial. 15.11.86 GOING TO WORK IN ENGLISH — practical advice for working in an English-speaking environment. (Support Material available).
SUNDAY	**POP WORDS** — series explaining the words of pop songs. 19.10.86 SPEAKING OF ENGLISH — magazine programme for teachers of English and advanced learners. 25.1.87 MIXED BAG — another look at language and culture in all its richness. 8.3.87 STUDIO 87 — entertaining magazine style series on issues of the moment. At GMT 12.15 TELLING TALES — original short stories set mainly in and around Britain. 15.11.86 WHAT TO SAY WHEN — ways of discussing everyday topics; how to give an opinion or make a deduction. 8.2.87 HOW TO LISTEN — a course teaching learners to improve their ability to listen to the speech of native speakers.	**CAN I HELP YOU?** — Repeat of Monday's transmission. 25.1.87 POP WORDS — series explaining the lyrics of pop songs.
MONDAY	**CAN I HELP YOU?** — answers to listeners' questions on English grammar and usage. 26.1.87 ENGLISH BY RADIO DEBATES — highlights and commentary based on public debates on issues in the learning and teaching of English.	**SPEAKING OF ENGLISH** — repeat of Sunday's broadcast. 26.1.87 PROFESSOR GRAMMAR a look at the rules of grammar; with exercises (repeat).
TUESDAY	**NOVEL CHOICE II** — new series looking at novels written by non-British authors. 25.11.86 CONFESSIONS — five short plays, with explanations of the language used. In each play one of the characters confesses to something that has been important in his or her life. 6.1.87 PICKWICK PAPERS — a dramatisation, with explanations, of one of Charles Dickens' most famous novels.	**TALKING ABOUT POETRY** — an analysis of seventeen poems with readings and explanations. 3.2.87 LORD OF THE MANOR — an old fashioned romance in a popular and 'corny' style.
WEDNESDAY	**PROFESSOR GRAMMAR** — a look at the rules of grammar; with exercises. 10.12.86 THINKING — thoughts, which lead to practice of points of grammar. 18.2.87 CONVERSATION PIECES — the English you need for general conversation.	**CONVERSATION PIECES** — the English you need for general conversation. 14.1.87 PUT IT IN WRITING — listening and writing practice. 18.3.87 TAKE THIS DOWN — a series of dictations based around a newspaper office.
THURSDAY	**COUNCILLOR CARTER** — upper intermediate series on Britain's system of local government. Plus (6.11.86) ENGLISH BY RADIO NEWS REVIEW* — a review of some of the major events of the week. Broadcast in special English. 27.11.86 LESSONS IN HISTORY — people or events in history that have changed British society and, often, had a significance in the wider world; plus THE NEWS QUIZ* — a quiz about world events of 1986; followed by NEWS REVIEW*. 5.2.87 LESSONS IN LOGIC.	**TALKING SHOP** — the language of business, set in one of London's most famous department stores. 18.12.86 TALKING CARS — series teaching business language, concentrating on the manufacture of the Maestro. 12.3.87 FINANCIAL ENGLISH — a course in the specialist field of finance and banking.
FRIDAY	**THE FINAL YEAR** — is there life after school? Students of a British Comprehensive school prepare themselves for the world outside the classroom. 26.12.86 THREE PANTOMIMES — special programmes for Christmas. 16.1.87 THE FINAL YEAR.	**HOMEWORK** — the language and concepts behind The Final Year. 26.12.86 THE LANGUAGE OF PANTOMIME — The language used in the Christmas pantomime programmes. 16.1.87 THE FINAL YEAR.

*The English by Radio News Review and The News Quiz (see Thursday) will be on all transmissions from 11.30 to 11.45 and 21.45 to 22.00.

When to Listen ...

The programme times are given in Greenwich Mean Time (GMT). To calculate the equivalent clock times for your own country it may be necessary to add some hours as follows:

Austria, Belgium, Czechoslavakia, Denmark, France, Germany, Hungary, Italy, Luxembourg, Malta, Netherlands, Norway, Poland, Spain, Sweden, Yugoslavia, Switzerland — add 1 hour. Bulgaria, Cyprus (Ercan), Cyprus (Larnaca), Finland, Greece, Romania, Turkey — add 2 hours. U.S.S.R. — add 3 hours from Kiev, Leningrad, Moscow, Odessa. Add an additional 1 hour approximately for each 15 degrees longitude east in U.S.S.R.

How to tune in ...

BBC English by Radio lessons are broadcast on the MEDIUM WAVE (MW) and SHORT WAVE Bands. You probably use the MEDIUM WAVE Band for listening to your own country's radio. On your radio dial MEDIUM WAVE is divided into metres (m) and/ or Kilohertz (kHz) like this ... (463/648 kHz is demonstrated).

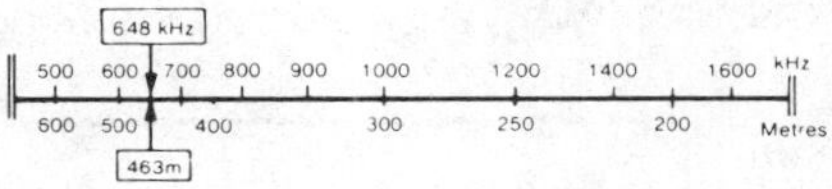

To tune in to the lessons broadcast on the SHORT WAVE Band you will have to adjust the tuning of your radio after pressing a button or turning a switch. Depending on where your radio was made the following letters may indicate the SHORT WAVE Band — K, C, OC or S. SHORT WAVE is divided into metres/metrebands (m) and megahertz (MHz) and may look something like this on your radio dial ...

The arrows show where to find the following frequencies:

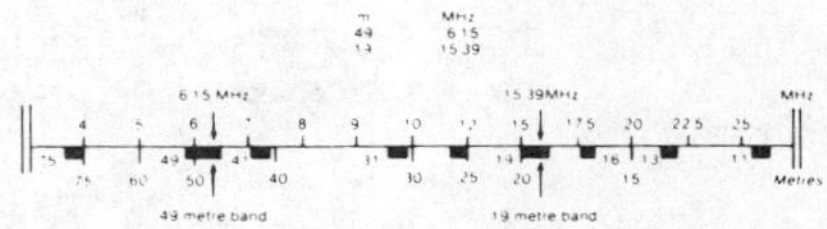

We have illustrated the whole of the SHORT WAVE Band. Most radio sets include only part of this waveband.

The information above applies to radio sets where the tuning indicator is exactly on target. It is possible for radio sets to go off target with age or rough treatment. If you have difficulty in picking up BBC English by Radio lessons at the points on the dial we have suggested it might be worth moving the tuning control very carefully either side of the point indicated. It is best if you can have your set checked by a radio engineer who would confirm whether or not the tuning control is on target.

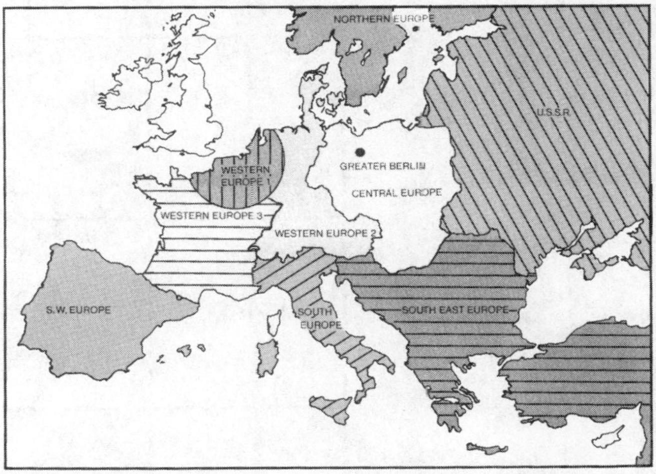

WESTERN EUROPE: 1.

0645-0700	6.195, 3.975, 1296kHz, 648kHz
0730-0745	6.195, 3.975, 1296kHz
1215-1230 (Sun)	6.125, 3.955, 1296kHz
1230-1300	6.125, 1296kHz
1715-1745	7.165, 6.185, 3.975, 648kHz
2130-2200	7.14, 6.03
2245-2300	1296kHz

WESTERN EUROPE: 2.

0645-0700	11.945, 7.26, 6.195, 6.15, 3.975, 1296kHz, 648kHz
1230-1300	15.39, 12.04, 7.32
1715-1745	7.165, 6.185, 3.975, 648kHz
2130-2200	7.14, 6.03
2245-2300	1296kHz

WESTERN EUROPE: 3.

0645-0700	11.945, 6.195, 3.975, 648kHz
0730-0745	9.915,7.23, 6.195, 3.975, 1296kHz
1230-1300	11.78, 9.66, 6.125
1715-1745	7.165, 6.185, 3.975, 648kHz
2130-2200	7.14, 6.03

NORTHERN EUROPE.

1230-1300	11.78, 7.32

SOUTH WEST EUROPE.

0730-0745	9.915, 7.23, 6.195, 3.975, 1296kHz
1230-1300	11.78. 9.66
1715-1745	7.165, 6.185, 3.975, 648kHz MW

SOUTH EAST EUROPE.

0530-0545	9.75, 7.285, 7.155, 6.14, 6.015, 3.99
1230-1300	15.39, 12.04, 9.635, 6.18
1845-1900	6.07
2130-2200	7.14, 6.03

SOUTH EUROPE.

0530-0545	9.75, 7.285, 7.155, 6.10
0645-0700	11.945, 7.26, 6.195, 3.975
1230-1300	15.39, 12.04
2130-2200	7.14, 6.03

CENTRAL EUROPE.

0530-0545	7.285, 7.155, 6.14, 6.015
0645-0700	11.945, 7.26, 6.15, 3.975, 1296kHz
1230-1300	15.39, 12.04, 7.32
2130-2200	7.235, 7.14, 6.03

U.S.S.R.

1230-1300	17.695, 15.27, 11.73, 9.605

GREATER BERLIN.

0530-0545	810kHz, 90.2
0645-0700	810kHz, 90.2
1715-1730	810kHz, 90.2

NOTE

For updated details of broadcasts, write to:
BBC English
Queens House
28 Kingsway
London WC2

Unit 12 Kicking The Habit

This unit is about cigarette smoking: why people start and how difficult it is to give it up.

1 Listen to Muriel and Cecil. Does Cecil smoke? How do you know?

2 Talk to the other students in the class and find out:
- if they smoke.
- how many cigarettes they smoke a day.
- what brand they smoke.

3 Copy the grid below. Then listen to the people on the tape talking about when and why they started smoking and fill in the grid.

	WHEN	WHY
STEVE		
MIRIAM		
ANNE		
JOHN		

4 Now talk to someone who smokes and find out when and why he or she started.

5 Look at this leaflet from the Health Education Council. On the tape you will hear different people giving reasons for giving up smoking. They mention some of the points mentioned in the leaflet and also add some that are not there. As you listen, match the reasons they give with the ones in the leaflet and make a note of any new ones that are not there.

The people you are going to hear are:

1 Mike and Liz
2 Miriam
3 Alison
4 Christopher and Anne
5 Muriel
6 Muriel and Cecil
7 Miriam

Nobody pretends that giving up smoking is easy. But a lot of people have managed it, and so could you.

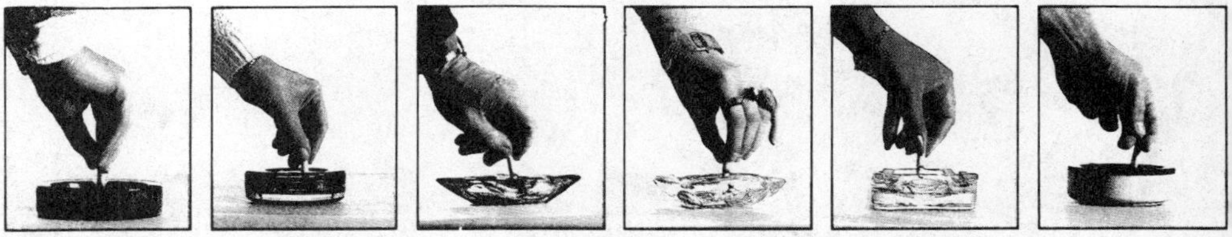

Here are some of the reasons for giving up:

- Cigarette smoking increases your risk of lung cancer which kills over 38,000 people in the United Kingdom every year. **That's one every 14 minutes.**
- Smoking increases your risk of heart disease. The average smoker is about **twice as likely** to die of a heart attack than a non-smoker.
- The average smoker is much more likely to develop chronic bronchitis – a crippling lung disease which kills **over 24,000 people a year.**
- Out of every 1,000 young people who smoke, six will be killed in traffic accidents but **250 will be killed by smoking.**
- In this country **every year** 50,000 people die before their time because of smoking.
- On average a smoker shortens his life by about **5½ minutes** for each cigarette smoked.

Here's what you'll gain when you do give up:

- Your chances of avoiding a heart attack,. bronchitis and lung cancer will start to improve.
- You won't be so short of breath.
- You'll help that smoker's cough.
- No more yellow fingers and teeth.
- Your breath, your hair and your clothes stop smelling of stale tobacco.
- If you are pregnant, your baby will stand a better chance of being born healthy.
- Your children will be less likely to smoke.
- You'll save money.

There's a booklet that will help you give up called 'The Smoker's Guide to Non-Smoking.' You can get a copy from your local Health Education Service, or from The Health Education Council, 78 New Oxford Street, London WC1A 1AH.

LOOK AFTER YOURSELF!

6 The people you listened to in task 5 used the following phrasal verbs. Listen to the tape again. Listen carefully for the verbs below and write down a word or expression that means the same.

Mike/Liz: *gave up*

Miriam: *give up*
went up
took up
get through
went back

Alison: *give up*

Christopher/Anne: *go back*

Muriel: *gave up*
went off

Muriel/Cecil: *give up*
take up
take on

Miriam: *carrying on*

7 All of the people you listened to have given up or tried to give up smoking. On the left are some ways of encouraging people to give it up. What do you think of them? Which are the most effective?

SOME SUCCESSFUL STOP SMOKING PROGRAMMES

Efforts to reduce smoking have included:

- government restrictions on cigarette advertising
- no-smoking areas in public places
- anti-smoking advertisements
- stop smoking groups, TV programmes and publications
- school programmes
- advice from health professionals.

Now read what the authorities say. Do their findings agree with what you thought?

WHICH OF THESE METHODS HAS HAD MOST EFFECT?

- Although advertising campaigns alone have not led to great changes in smoking behaviour they continue to play an important role. As a result of the recent 'Superman' campaign aimed at 7-11 year old children, 600,000 children wrote to the Health Education Council to join the fight against the evil 'Nick O'Teen'.
- Smoking cessation groups have produced an average stop smoking rate after one year of 15%. Work continues with stop smoking groups in order to find more successful methods. The evaluation of these groups has also helped us understand more about when and why people smoke and the difficulties they have in stopping. The results show however that most people who stop are not attending a formal stop smoking group.
- Researchers are also looking at the use of nicotine gum, and examining the combination of behaviour change methods which can produce higher stop smoking rates. These methods include making a contract to stop smoking with someone else (verbal or financial), being aware of the situations in which you smoke and trying to change them, and promoting the idea that smoking is unattractive and distasteful.
- Recent school programmes have resulted in a measurable change in the number of adolescents who start to smoke. These new programmes are still being tested but they have already increased our understanding of some of the reasons behind teenage smoking. The key factors seem to be pressure from friends and the example set by parents, siblings and important adults.
- In one study, advice from a doctor to give up smoking, together with back-up material and a warning of a possible 'follow-up' resulted in 5% of a healthy group of people stopping smoking. In another study anti-smoking advice was given to smokers at high risk of cardiorespiratory disease. After 10 years the group who had received advice were smoking half as many cigarettes as the control group. There is no reason why nurses shouldn't have the same success.
- In Finland and the USA a significant reduction in the number of smokers was produced by a combination of mass media programmes, environmental changes and advice from health professionals.

So it would seem that there is no one programme at the moment which can be effective on its own. Instead, a variety of approaches, co-ordinated with each other and directed both at the individual and at society as a whole, have produced the best results.

Unit 13 Getting Your Tongue Round It

This unit is about languages and their sounds. You will hear people saying what languages they find attractive, and why. You will also hear someone talking about how important they feel pronunciation to be in a foreign language and how to make it better. You will also be able to think about how you work on your own pronunciation in English.

1 Look at the words in the box and try to pair them up in opposites or near opposites. They will be useful for the tasks in this unit.

loud **passionate**
quiet **harsh**
soft **noisy**
prosaic **dull**
romantic **tender**

2 Listen to these four people. What languages are they speaking? How do the different languages sound to you – are they pleasant, attractive, soft, musical, etc.? (Try to use some of the words from task 1.)

3 What languages appeal to you because of how they sound? If you can, work with a partner and explain what it is that appeals to you.

4 Listen to these people talking about how they think different foreign languages sound or how they think foreign accents in English sound. Make a note of the languages and accents and what the people think about how they sound.

The people you are going to hear are:

1 Iain
2 Chris
3 Donald
4 Lesley
5 Ravi
6 Peter

5 Read this text from *A Room with a View* by E.M. Forster and answer the following questions.

a Do you agree with what he says about the sound of Italian when spoken by an Italian?

b Does he like the way Mr Eager speaks Italian? How do you know?

> Mr Eager, who suffered from an overfluent tongue rather than a resolute will, was determined to make himself heard. He addressed the driver again. Italian in the mouth of Italians is a deep-voiced stream, with unexpected cataracts and boulders to preserve it from monotony. In Mr Eager's mouth it resembled nothing so much as an acid whistling fountain which played ever higher and higher, and quicker and quicker, and more and more shrilly, till abruptly it was turned off with a click.

6 Which foreign accent do you like in your own language? Think about why you like it and then tell a partner.

7 Do you think it is important to try to perfect your pronunciation in the language you are learning? Listen to Lesley, who is a language teacher and a language learner, talking about this. Answer these questions.

a Does she think it is important to try to develop good pronunciation? Why?

b What does she say about her pronunciation in Spanish?

c What two ways of improving pronunciation does she mention?

d Does she agree with what these writers say?

> MOST . . . language learners need no more than a comfortably intelligible pronunciation (and by "comfortably" intelligible I mean a pronunciation which can be understood with little or no conscious effort on the part of the listener).

> The basic strategy is *imitation* of utterances (sentences, phrases, etc.) supplemented by practice in specific problem areas.

8 Work either individually or in groups and think or talk about the importance you give to good pronunciation. Give reasons. Then make a list of all the ways you think you can improve your pronunciation. (Lesley has given you two already!) If you find it easier, you could think of a particular sound you have problems with in English and list all the ways you could work on it.

9 Look at this tongue-twister. Can you say it?

She sells sea shells on the sea shore.
The shells that she sells are sea shells I'm sure.

Now listen to this English person trying to say it. What are the sounds that she finds difficult?

Practise saying it again, or try this other one:

Peter Piper picked a peck of pickled pepper.
A peck of pickled pepper Peter Piper picked.
If Peter Piper picked a peck of pickled pepper
where's the peck of pickled pepper Peter Piper picked?

10 One of the problems with English is that spelling does not closely reflect pronunciation. This text gives an example:

Pronunciation is not based on spelling. Language is primarily an oral phenomenon, and in many respects (but not in every respect), the written form can be considered as a kind of representation of the spoken. Ideally, the spelling system should closely reflect pronunciation, and in many languages, that indeed is the case. But, alas, it is not the case in English. English spelling is only a poor reflection of English pronunciation, although it must be admitted that there are many regularities between sound and written symbol which it is valuable for the teacher to know.

The nature of the problem is twofold: firstly, each sound of English is represented by more than one written letter or by sequences of letters; and secondly, any letter of English represents more than one sound, or it may not represent any sound at all. The most familiar example of the lack of consistency between spelling and pronunciation is the letter sequence *ough*. Test for yourself the variations that this letter sequence represents in spelling:

though	(rhymes with *slow*)	*cough*	(rhymes with *off*)
through	(rhymes with *true*)	*tough*	(rhymes with *stuff*)
thought	(rhymes with *taut*)	*bough*	(rhymes with *now*)
thorough	(rhymes partially with *colour*)	*hough*	(rhymes with *lock*)

Now think of the letter '*o*'. Make a list of all the words you can think of where it is pronounced in different ways.

Unit 14 The Answering Machine

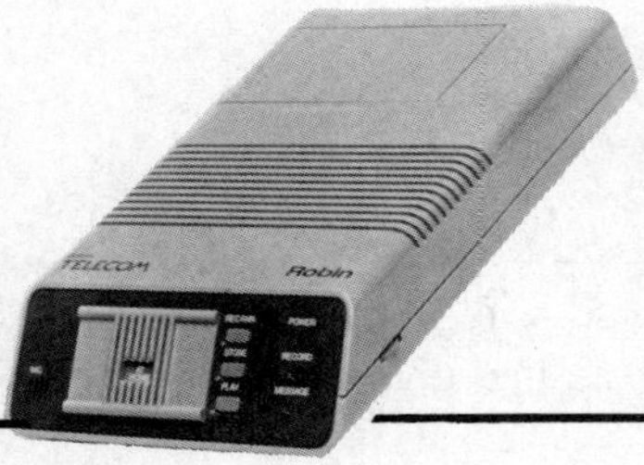

It is becoming more and more common, when phoning people up, to find that they have an answering machine. When it happens to you, what do you do? Do you leave a message or put the phone down without saying anything?

In this unit you will listen to messages that different people have left on answering machines.

After just a few days using the new Robin telephone answering and recording machine, it'll become as integral to your lifestyle as your telephone itself. What's more, with its many advanced features and refreshingly low price, you'll begin to wonder why everyone doesn't have one.

Because, as you'll never miss a call from a friend or relative, your social life becomes far more organised. You can go to work, go out for a meal, even relax in the bath and know that the Robin will record all incoming calls for you to play back later.

Despite its low price, the Robin doesn't skimp on features.

There's a light that tells you if you have any messages.

A button for keeping messages for future listening.

And a remote interrogation facility that allows you to hear your messages from a telephone anywhere in the world (unlike some machines, you don't need a bleeper to do this).

What's more, the Robin is extremely simple to operate – easier, in fact, than a portable cassette player. And it comes with everything you need to start using it immediately – a C60 cassette tape, transformer, and doubler socket. Full instructions are also provided.

1 Listen to these four messages. Who are the messages for and what do the callers want?

2 Steve Todd runs a small Japanese/English translating business from his home in London. Listen to these messages that he found on his answering machine one evening.

Who is phoning and what do they want?

3 Now *you* call Steve and leave some messages on his machine. (Record your messages on a tape recorder if you have one.) First, read the three situations below. Before you leave the messages, think about what you are going to say, but *don't* write anything down.

a You work for a translation agency and you receive this request.

P.P.A. Industrial PLC,
243 Oxford Rd,
Reading,
Berks.
Tel. 44623, 44624, 44625

Despatch Translations,
444 Charlotte Street,
London. W1

2.4.87

Dear Mr Peake,

Ref. no. JSH/TECH/177

Further to our telephone conversation of today, please find enclosed seven pages of technical Japanese for translation.

Please return completed scripts by the end of the month, quoting our reference number.

We look forward to hearing from you.

Yours sincerely,

J.S. HOLLAND

b You are given two tickets for a play tomorrow evening and you would like to go with Steve.

c You are a bit bored and you just want to chat.

4 Listen to the tape for task 2 again. The different callers ask Steve to telephone them but they use different words and expressions to say it. Write down all the different ways of saying 'telephone me' that you hear.

5 If you have your own answering machine, you have to leave a message to identify yourself when people telephone. What message would you leave on your answering machine?

Unit 15 The Selection Board

In this unit you will hear someone being interviewed for a job as an English language teacher. As well as listening to the language, you will also look at the kinds of gesture and body language used and think about different teaching styles.

1 Read these two advertisements for English language teachers to work with the British Council in the United Arab Emirates. What differences are there between the two posts?

1

United Arab Emirates

Two Teachers of English, British Council, Dubai

Duties: to teach English at all levels and to assist, if required, on the RSA Prep Cert. Other duties include assistance with syllabus construction and revision, registration and student placement, UCLES and RSA examinations.
Qualifications: degree, RSA Dip TEFL or equivalent, at least 2 years' TEFL experience. Candidates should be single or a married teaching couple without children.
Salary: 5,000 Dhs per month (£1– approx Dhs 5.3).
Benefits: free furnished accommodation, 8 weeks' annual leave, air fares, baggage allowance, terminal gratuity, medical scheme.
Contract: one year from September, renewable by mutual agreement.
Reference: 85 D 95-96 T

2

United Arab Emirates

Three Teachers of English, The British Council, Abu Dhabi

Duties: to teach English to adults at all levels, co-ordination responsibilities, student registration.
Qualifications: degree, RSA Dip TEFL or PGCE (TEFL); at least 2 years' TEFL experience. Candidates should be single or a married teaching couple.
Salary: 5,000 Dhs per month (£1–approx 5.3 Dhs).
Benefits: free furnished accommodation, eight weeks' annual leave, airfares, baggage allowance, gratuity, medical scheme.
Contract: one year from September, renewable by mutual agreement.
Reference: 85 D 92-94 T

2 Laurie Thomas is an English language teacher working in the Middle East. He recently applied for the above posts and was shortlisted and invited to an interview. Read the following questions, and then listen to this extract from his interview.

- **a** What type of students does Laurie have most experience with?
- **b** Why is he applying for these posts?
- **c** Which of the two posts is he more suitable for?

3 Read the following questions, and then listen to Laurie talking to Amy, a friend, about the interview.

a How does he feel he performed?

b How many other candidates were there?

c Would you say he was confident or pessimistic? Why?

4 Look at these four photographs of Laurie. Which, do you think, were taken during his interview? Give reasons for your answers.

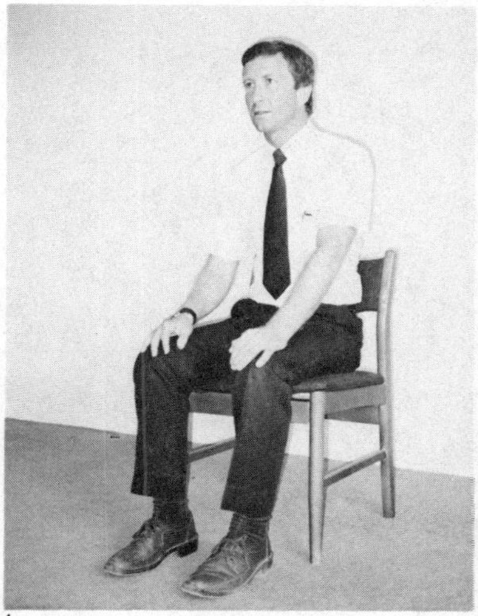

1

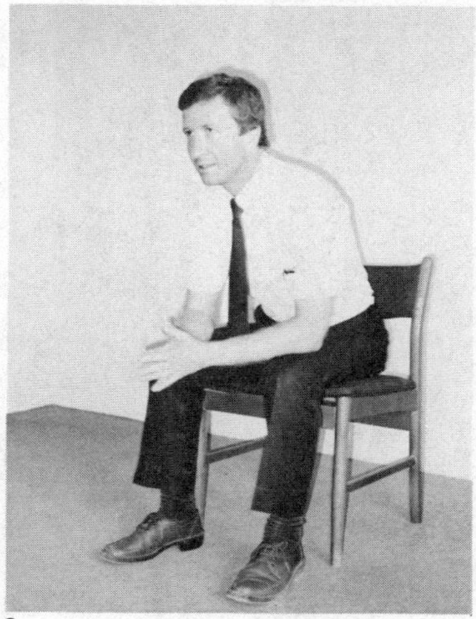

2

3

4

5 Amy says very little to Laurie (task 3) besides '*uh, huh*', '*mmm...*' Listen again and decide what these noises mean.

Say '*mmm...*' in different ways to mean different things.

For example: pleasure suspicion surprise

6 Can you think of other ways of communicating without using words? Make a list.

7 Here are some common gestures used in the English-speaking world. What do they mean? Do they mean the same in your culture?

1

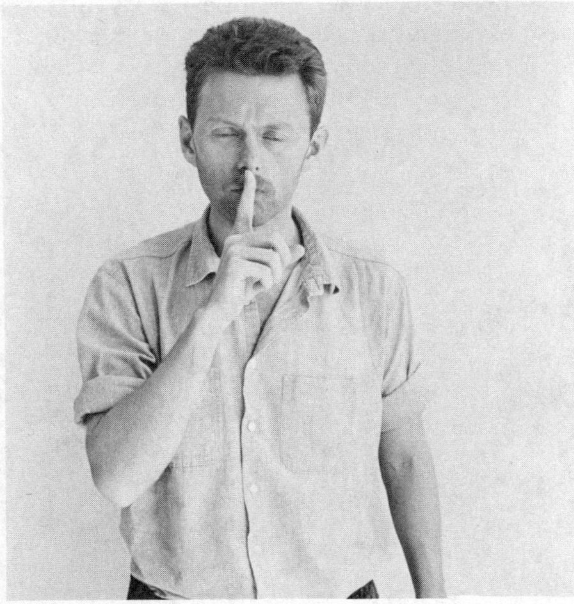

2

3

4

8 People in Britain who are born profoundly deaf or who go deaf in early childhood communicate by using visual/gestural language called British sign language. This language uses all parts of the body to communicate, i.e. face, gesture, posture, lip patterns and hands, and fingerspelling. Here is the British two-hand manual alphabet. Form pairs or groups and send messages to other groups.

9 Work in small groups and discuss what you think should be the role of the teacher in the classroom. You might find it helpful to refer to the extracts from the trainee teachers' examination answers in task 7 in the unit called 'Learning How: Learning? How?'

Here are some questions to get you started.

- Who should decide what is to be taught?
- Who should decide how a thing is to be taught?
- Who is responsible for learning?
- Who should be doing most of the talking?
- Where should the teacher stand or sit?

10 Here is another extract from Laurie's interview. Read the following questions and then listen to the tape.

a What do Middle Eastern students expect from their teachers?

b How are 'the modern teaching techniques which are used in Europe' different?

Unit 16 A Diplomatic Frieze

This unit contains part of an official taped guide to the British Museum in London. What do you know about the British Museum? Have you ever been there or have you read anything about it? Do you know where any of the exhibits are from?

1 In many museums you can hire a taped guide in your own language. Here is part of the English guide to the Duveen Gallery at the British Museum. Copy the ground plan of the gallery below, listen to the tape, and complete the annotation.

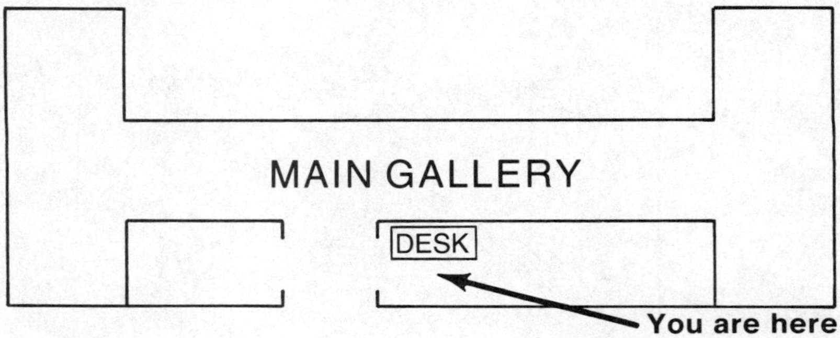

2 Now answer these questions. Listen to the tape again if you need to.

a Who was Lord Elgin?

b What are the 'Elgin Marbles'?

c Who was responsible for building the Parthenon and when was it built?

d Who designed the statue of Athena?

3 The Parthenon frieze is housed in the main gallery. Here are two sections from the frieze. They each show a centaur (half-man, half-horse) and a Lapith (hillsman). Listen to this part of the guide and decide which picture is being described.

1

2

4 Here is a picture of some figures. They are all gods and goddesses. Some have been named. Listen to the tape and note down the other names.

5 Here is a newspaper article about the Elgin Marbles. Read it and make a note of the arguments for and against returning the 'Elgin Marbles' to Greece.

Marbles plea 'will never be given up'

THE Greek Minister of Culture, Miss Melina Mercouri, made an impassioned plea last night for the return of the Elgin Marbles held by the British Museum.

She told students at the Oxford Union: "England and Greece are friends, and it is in the spirit of this friendship that we say there was an injustice that can now be corrected."

She rejected the British definition of them as the Elgin Marbles, and said they were the Parthenon Marbles, whose removal involved wanton devastation.

"My Government has asked for their return and we have been refused. But we shall never abandon this request."

Miss Mercouri rejected claims that returning the marbles to Greece could set a precedent leading to the emptying of museums all over the world.

She said: "This is just plain rubbish. Museums are vital social and cultural assets and must be protected. But we are asking for the return of an integral part of a structure that was mutilated.

"We are asking for the return of something unique to Greece and specific to our identity. I believe that such a gesture from Britain would ever honour your name."

Miss Mercouri was speaking before the start of a debate on a motion "That the Elgin Marbles must be returned to Greece."

6 Now listen to Miss Rankine, deputy director of the British Museum, talking about the Elgin Marbles. What does she think of the Greek claim?

7 What do *you* think should be done with the Elgin Marbles? If you can, work in groups and discuss the arguments you have listened to on the tape.

8 Visit a local museum and find out where its exhibits come from. Should any of the exhibits be returned to their country of origin?

9 Look at this photograph of the painting 'St George and the Dragon', by Paolo Uccello. Listen to the museum guide for task 4 again and use it as a model to produce a guide for the exhibit shown on the photograph. Record your commentary on a cassette player, if you can, and either listen to it yourself or exchange it with someone else in the class. As you listen, try to notice some of these things:

- the speed: is it fast, slow or just right?
- the pronunciation.
- the intonation.
- the amount of information.

Paolo UCCELLO (c. 1397–1475).
St George and the Dragon.

Unit 17 Dial A Line

The material in this unit is based on the recorded information that British Telecom, the British telephone company, provides to subscribers.

1 Work in pairs or small groups if possible, and make a list of the telephone services available in your country or city.

2 Look at this page from the British Telecom code book which lists services for the London area. Listen to the tape and note down the names of the services you hear.

Guidelines

information services

BRITISH GAS RECIPELINE	
a different recipe each day	
Monday – Friday *8am - 6pm*	246 8071
CAPITAL RADIOLINE	
Tune into your favourite programmes for Capital Radio	246 8024
CHALLENGELINE	
Daily brain-teasers: *answers given the following day*	246 8050
CHILDREN'S LONDON	
Events and competitions	246 8007
DAILY EXPRESS CRICKETLINE	
During Test Matches played in England and other major matches *8am - 7pm*	154
DAILY MIRROR TELEFUN SHOW	
Humorous entertainment	246 8070
EVENTLINE	
Motor sport information	246 8066
FT CITYLINE	
For business news and FT index	246 8026
For international market reports	246 8086
GOLDEN HITLINE	
Hits from the 60's and 70's	246 8044
I.R.N. NEWSLINE	
News bulletin updated hourly	246 8080
LEISURELINE	
Daily selection of main events in and around London	
In English	246 8041
In French	246 8043
In German	246 8045
Edinburgh: *1 May-30 Sept*	031-246 8041
NATIONAL SUMMARIES	
Air	246 8033
Rail *(Inter City and London Service)*	246 8030
Road *(Motorways and Major Trunk Roads)*	246 8031
Sea	246 8032
PUFFIN STORYLINE	
Bedtime stories from 6pm each night	246 8000
SKILINE *1 Dec-30 April but may be extended*	
Skiing conditions at the principal Scottish ski-centres	031-246 8031
SPACELINE	
Space mission information	246 8055
SPORTSLINE	
General sports round-up	246 8020
STARLINE *for your daily horoscope*	
6am - 6pm daily	246 8000
TIMELINE *for the speaking clock*	
24 hour service	123
TRAVELINE *Road, Rail, Air and Sea Service*	
Birmingham *(50 mile radius)*	021-246 8021
Bristol *(70 mile radius)*	Bristol (0272) 8021
Liverpool *(50 mile radius)*	051-246 8021
London *(70 mile radius)*	246 8021
Northern England	Newcastle-upon-Tyne (0632) 8021
Northern Ireland	Belfast (0232) 8021
Scotland	031-246 8021
South & West Yorkshire	Leeds (0532) 8021

3 Copy this chart. Listen to F.T. Cityline again and fill in the foreign exchange rates for £ sterling.

£1 =

	US $.
	D.Mark
	S. Franc
	Yen

4 Look at the map below and match the following words with the numbers on the map:

junction **southbound** **contraflow**

intersection **flyover**

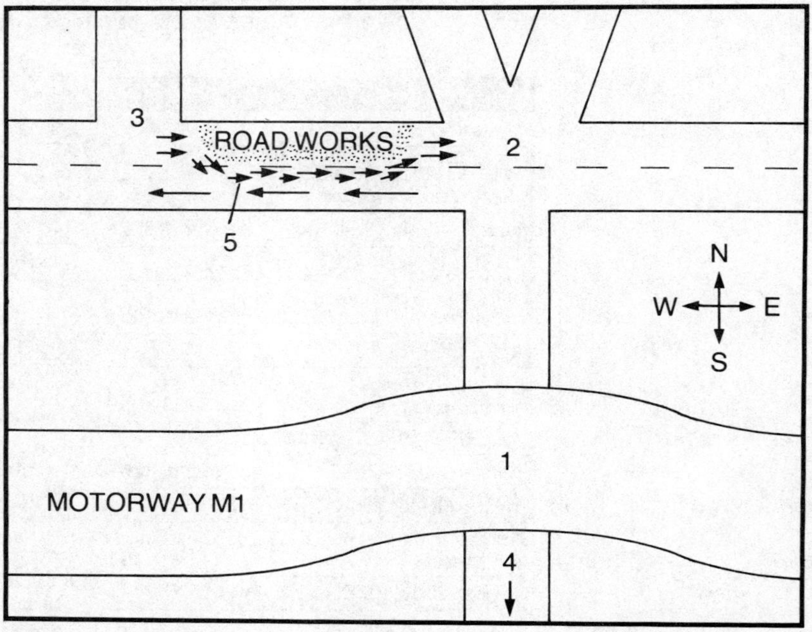

5 Look at these maps and listen to Traveline again. What areas, roads, or junctions should you try to avoid if you were in a car?

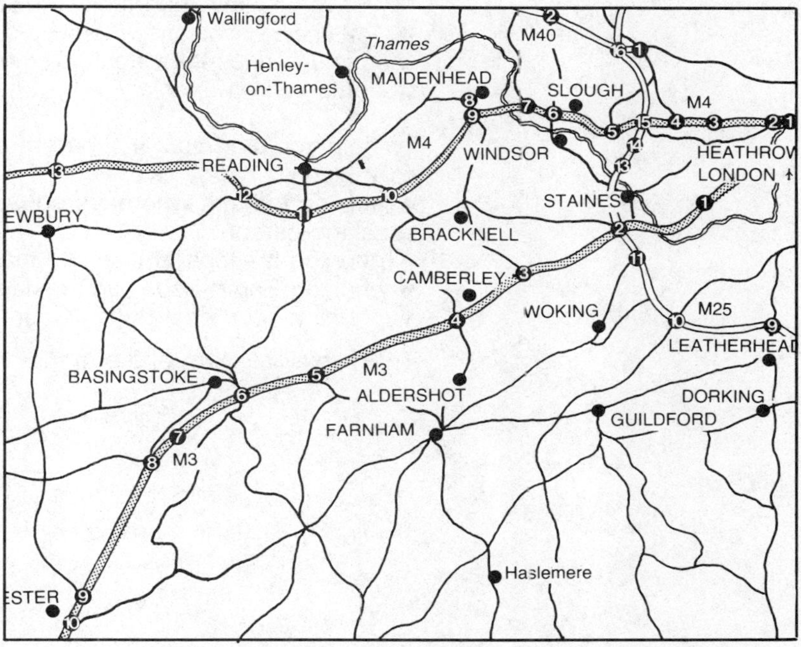

1

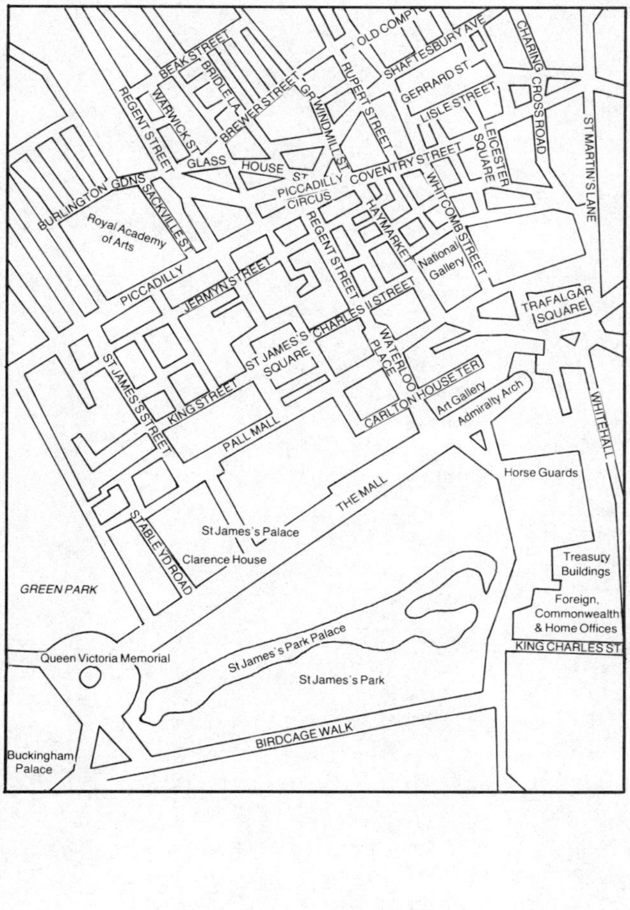

2

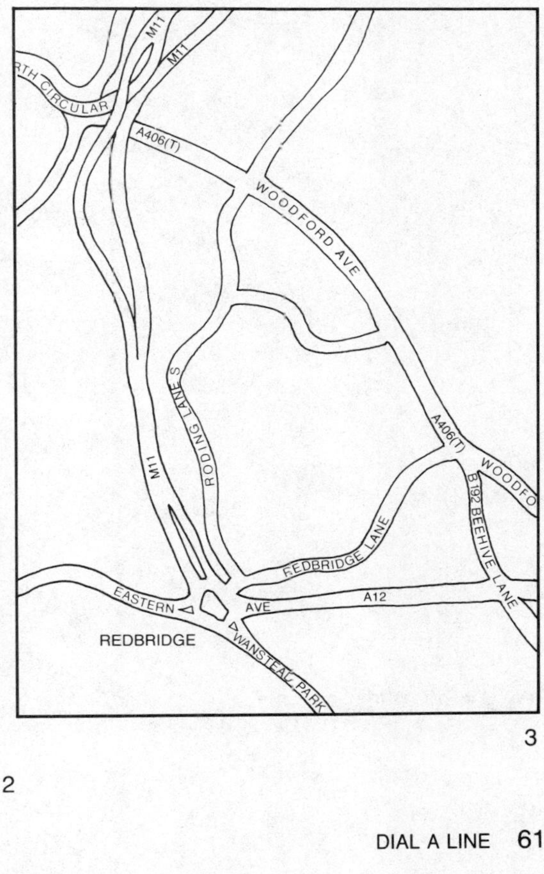

3

6 Listen to London Leisureline again and then prepare and record a message for leisure activities in and around your town.

7 Have you any opportunity to use the telephone in English? Think of all the occasions when you could do so and make a list. Then choose one and make a call after the class. Report back to the other students in the next class.

To help you start your list, here are some possible occasions:
- at work.
- helping a friend who does not speak English to call an English-speaking person.
- phoning the local British or American Consulate for information.
- phoning English-speaking residents in your town.
- phoning your local British Council office for information.

Try to think of more and add them to the list.

Acknowledgements

The authors would like to thank the following people for allowing their voices to be used on the tape:

Fiona Abbott, Bridget Anfossy, Roger Beckett, Martin Blasall, Peter Boag, Judith Brown, Christopher Caldwell, Nicky Cameron, Dorrie Chetty, Simon Clackson, Anne Clackson, Susanna Clarke, Lesley Denham, Christine Doye, Elizabeth Duff, Dave Fischer, Amy Fishburn, Gemma Gallart, Christopher Greenland, Sunil Gupta, John Hart, Victoria Hellier, William Herschell, Tina Hopkins, David Kellock, Pat Lynch, Alison Madgwick, Tim Madgwick, David Mann, Deborah Manning, Nigel Marsh, Donald McDowall-Wilson, Peter Moran, Joy Morris, Ruth Myott, Annie Nicol, Ravi Phull, David Poole, Mike Rigby, Jean Rankine, Laurence Thomas, Mary Tallon, Steve Todd, Brenda Ward, Alison Wertheimer, Cecil Wonham, Chuck Wunderman, and 'Kyoko'.

We would also like to thank Andrew Hamilton (Press Officer, British Museum), Mr Bridger (from Lloyd's), and Peter Hart for their help, and the British Council for allowing us to record one of their interviews.

The publishers would like to thank the following for their permission to reproduce copyright material:

Ahlan Wasahlan for Curtis Casewit: *The Art of Handwriting Analysis*; Albery Theatre for tickets; Edward Arnold for E M Forster: *A Room with a View*; BBC World Service for part of the 'Learn English' leaflet; The British Council for two advertisements which were placed in *The Times Educational Supplement* of 24 January 1986; The British Deaf Association for the British two-handed manual alphabet; British Telecom for part of the code book and Robin telephone answering and recording machine advertisement, and for extracts from their telephone information services; *Building* for part of an article about Lloyd's; Executive Post for 'Language – the key to export marketing'; Health Education Council for extracts from 'Look after yourself', 'Why I stopped smoking' and 'The facts about smoking'; Hi-fi News & Record Review for a review; Longman Group Limited for D Abercrombie: *Problems and Principles in Language Study 2nd edition*; Macmillan Publishers for P Tench: *Pronunciation Skills*; Metropolitan Police Office for parts of Form 966a; Penguin for *Penguin Dictionary of Psychology*, George Orwell: *1984*; M Drabble: *The Ice Age* and The Press Association for the article 'Marbles plea "will never be given up"'.

The publishers would like to thank the following for their permission to reproduce copyright photographs:

Jordi Puig, p.8; AVUI Newspaper, Barcelona, p.17; British Telecom, p.50 top; The British Museum, pp.56, 57; The National Gallery, p.58.

The photographs on pages 9, 16, 20, 21, 28, 24, 30, 35, 50 bottom, 52, 54 have been supplied by the authors.